Best Easy Day Hikes
Zion and Bryce Canyon National Parks

Help Us Keep This Guide Up to Date

Every effort has been made by the author and editors to make this guide as accurate and useful as possible. However, many things can change after a guide is published—trails are rerouted, regulations change, facilities come under new management, and so forth.

We appreciate hearing from you concerning your experiences with this guide and how you feel it could be improved and kept up to date. While we may not be able to respond to all comments and suggestions, we'll take them to heart, and we'll also make certain to share them with the author. Please send your comments and suggestions to the following address:

FalconGuides
Reader Response/Editorial Department
246 Goose Lane
Guilford, CT 06437

Or you may e-mail us at:

editorial@Falcon.com

Thanks for your input, and happy trails!

Best Easy Day Hikes Series

Best Easy Day Hikes Zion and Bryce Canyon National Parks

Second Edition

Erik Molvar and Tamara Martin

FALCONGUIDES

GUILFORD, CONNECTICUT
HELENA, MONTANA

Contents

Acknowledgments

First of all, we would like to thank the residents of Long Valley for their outstanding hospitality during the course of our research. Myrna Cox and her family, of Glendale, were particularly helpful in our search for a place to live. Thanks also to Cleve and Lorene Esplin and to the Chamberlains for sharing their fascinating stories with us. Steven Robinson was a wellspring of information about Cedar Breaks National Monument. Thanks also to Rod Schipper of the Bureau of Land Management's Kanab office for his geological insights. Dan Habig of Zion National Park provided interpretive information for this book, and Jerry Davis oversaw the review process for that part of the book. Thanks to Paula Henrie of Bryce Canyon National Park for reviewing the Bryce Canyon section. We would also like to thank our respective families, particularly Kathy, James, John, and Ginger, for their never-ending patience, support, and love throughout all of our adventures.

Introduction

The southwestern corner of Utah offers some of the most fascinating and awe-inspiring landscapes in the desert Southwest. Towering cliffs and slickrock canyons, with colorful spires and natural arches, exist here on a scale that dwarfs the works of humans and provides a humbling time scale by which to measure our own histories. Half a billion years in the making, this land was laid down in seas and lakes and dunes, then thrust skyward to be sculpted by the ceaseless efforts of wind and water. Here the visitor finds refuge from the fast-paced modern world, in a country little changed for a thousand years.

Weather

Southwestern Utah encompasses low deserts, arid uplands, and high, subalpine forestlands. There is no time of year when good hiking opportunities cannot be had.

Winters are cool and rainy at the lower elevations, but the high plateaus are typically locked in deep snowdrifts from November through April. Despite the snow, Bryce Canyon National Park is open year-round. Some of its day-hiking trails may remain passable throughout the winter, but deep snows collect in other areas.

Cedar Breaks and the rest of the Markagunt Plateau are completely snowbound and inaccessible to hikers during the winter. The uplands of Zion National Park typically are closed to entry during winter, although the Zion Canyon area remains open. Water temperatures are usually too low during winter to allow wading for extended periods.

The hallmark of spring is melting snow. Streams in this otherwise desert region become swollen with runoff, making many of the canyon hikes impassable. The high country is still snowbound at this time, although the Kolob Terrace of Zion National Park begins to open up in late April. The low deserts receive much of their annual rainfall in the spring, when they burst into a colorful display of blossoms. However, the moist soils of the low desert are prone to sticky mud at this time, which makes cross-country hiking an unpleasant activity—as well as one that can damage the environment. Spring is an excellent time to visit Bryce Canyon: Its cliffs and hoodoos are even prettier with a light dusting of snow.

Sweltering summer temperatures make hiking at midday toilsome, especially in the lower elevations. Confine your hiking to early morning and evening hours to avoid the worst of the heat. Savvy hikers retreat into the shady depths of the canyons or up to the breezy subalpine country atop the plateaus to beat the heat. The region experiences dry weather through the first half of summer, but late August is known for torrential thunderstorms that can trigger flash floods in the slot canyons and create spectacular waterfalls on the cliffs. Lightning strikes along the rims of the Bryce Canyon and Cedar Breaks amphitheaters are also a serious hazard at this time.

Autumn is perhaps the best time of year to visit the region. Temperatures are warm during the day, with frigid, crystal-clear nights. Water levels in the canyons are low at this time, and the water temperature remains fairly constant until late October, when it begins to plummet. As a bonus, travelers along the waterways are treated to colorful displays from the turning maples and cottonwoods, and visitors to the high country can take in the brilliant gold foliage of the aspens. The highest plateaus enjoy cool autumn weather but generally remain snow-free until mid-October. The lower terraces and canyon bottoms are warm and temperate at this time. Temperatures in the low desert of southwestern Zion become tolerable in late October.

Hiking in Arid Lands

Hiking in the Southwest poses challenges that are encountered nowhere else. Much of southwestern Utah's public land is free of trails, and hikers may have to rely on their map and compass skills to find their way. The defining feature of the region is "slickrock," in which vast expanses of sculpted sandstone have been scoured bare by wind and water. As its name suggests, slickrock can be very slippery when it gets wet. Trails and routes that cross slickrock will be marked only with cairns, if they are marked at all. Hikers who travel through canyons should remain constantly aware that it is much easier to climb up a slickrock face than it is to descend one.

Perhaps the most obvious challenge in desert hiking is the extreme weather. During the hottest parts of the day, the temperature can reach 120°F several feet above the floor of the low desert. Summer hikers should wear broad-brimmed hats, long-sleeved shirts, and baggy pants to protect themselves from the intensity of the desert sun. Cover exposed skin with sunscreen lotion. Take a lesson from the local wildlife—hike in the cool of the mornings and evenings, and rest in the shade during the heat of the day.

The desert air wicks moisture away from the body at an amazing rate, and active hikers should plan to drink about a gallon of water per day. Desert water sources may run dry for part of the year and often contain exotic microbes that can cause intestinal disorders. Always carry enough water to meet your daily needs, and filter all surface water before drinking to remove the harmful microbes.

Many desert-dwelling animals have evolved poisons, and they may bite or sting when provoked. The rattlesnake is the most notorious of these, although its reputation for aggressiveness is undeserved. This nocturnal predator will flee when given a chance, and it rarely bites unless it is surprised or cornered. To avoid snakebites, always watch where you put your hands and feet, and avoid reaching into dark places or overturning boulders. This practice will also help you avoid scorpions, most of which have painful stings. Scorpions like to hide in dark, moist places; hikers who leave their boots outside overnight may be in for a nasty surprise in the morning.

Desert hikers must be particularly careful not to upset the ecological balance of desert communities. Many plants and animals live on the edge of their capabilities, and any added stress may result in death. Give a wide berth to nesting birds, animals with young, and wildlife that is using a water source. Finally, hikers who are traveling in the low desert or piñon-juniper scrubland should avoid walking on biological soil crusts. These crusts are dark and granular and contain algae and other microbes that come alive following rains. A major source of nutrients for desert soils, they form a crucial link in the web of desert ecosystems. Biological soil crusts are very fragile and may not recover for decades after being trampled.

Sharing the Trail

Visitors should expect to encounter a wide variety of user groups in southwestern Utah, particularly on Bureau of

Land Management and National Forest lands. This magnificent wilderness is a magnet for outdoor folk and solitude seekers of all descriptions. In the interest of a safe and pleasant wilderness experience for all, exercise consideration and good manners when meeting other parties on the trail.

Pack and saddle stock have the right-of-way on the trails wherever they are allowed. Because pack and saddle stock are less maneuverable than foot travelers, hikers should yield to horse parties when the two meet on a trail. In such a situation, the best thing that a hiker can do is to hike up the hillside above the trail for at least 20 feet and allow the stock to pass. It often helps to talk to the animals in reassuring tones as they pass by. This keeps the animals from panicking and tangling up the pack string.

How to Follow a Faint Path

Many of the most popular treks in this corner of Utah exist only as primitive routes that may not be marked at all. Visitors to backcountry areas should have a few elementary trail-finding skills in their bag of tricks, in case a trail peters out or a snowfall covers the path. A topographic map and compass, and the ability to use them, are essential insurance against disaster when a trail takes a wrong turn or disappears completely.

Maintained trails in southwestern Utah are typically marked in a variety of ways. Signs bearing the name and/or number of the trail are present at some trail junctions, although weathering and inconsiderate visitors sometimes remove these plaques. Along the trail several kinds of markers indicate the location of maintained trails. In forested areas, cuts in the bark of living trees, known as blazes, are made immediately beside the path. In spots where a trail crosses a gravel streambed or bare slickrock, piles of rocks called cairns mark the route. These cairns are typically constructed of three or more stones piled atop one another, a formation that almost never occurs naturally.

In the case of an extremely overgrown trail, markings of any kind may be impossible to find. On such a trail the techniques used to build the trail serve as clues to its location. Well-constructed trails have rather wide, flat beds. Let your feet seek the flat spots when traveling through tall brush, and you will almost always find yourself on the trail. Look for check dams and other rock work on the trail that may have been put in place to prevent erosion. Old sawed logs from previous trail maintenance can be used to navigate in spots where the trail bed is obscured; if you find a sawed log, then you must be on a trail that was maintained at some point in time. Switchbacks are also a sure sign of an official trail; wild game travels in straight lines, and horsemen traveling off-trail seldom bother to zigzag across hillsides. Previous travelers can also leaves clues to the location of old trails; watch for footprints or hoof marks as you travel.

When attempting to find a trail that has disappeared, ask yourself where the most logical place would be to build a trail given its source and destination. Trail builders tend to seek level ground where it is available, and they often follow the natural contours of stream courses and ridgelines. Bear in mind that most trails avoid up-and-down motion in favor of long, sustained grades culminating in major passes or hilltops. Old trail beds can sometimes be spotted from a distance as they cut across hillsides at a constant angle.

Zero-Impact Camping Techniques for Arid Lands

Many backcountry areas in southwestern Utah do not have established camping areas. As a result, backpackers have unlimited options in choosing a spot to bed down. Along with this freedom comes the responsibility to leave the camping site exactly as it was found. It is easy to see that if even half of the backcountry campers left evidence of their passage, Utah's backcountry would soon be dotted with damaged campsites. Travelers should inspect their campsites when they leave and camouflage any spots that have been impacted. Pack out what you brought in with you, and pick up any trash that may have been left by less-considerate campers.

Campsite selection is a key component to an enjoyable backpacking trip. Choose a level spot that is already free of vegetation so that it doesn't have to be cleared. Flash floods are a very real threat to desert campers; even under blue skies, a rainstorm 20 miles away can send a wall of water down a dry wash in minutes. Be sure to pitch your camp on high ground, well away from stream courses. When traveling along a major canyon, do not camp in the mouth of a side canyon or across from its mouth: Flash floods that roar down tributary canyons typically expend much of their force in the area near the canyon's mouth. Finally, seeps and permanent streams are a critical feature of wildlife habitat. Camp at least 200 yards away from such water sources so that the animals will be undisturbed, and as a result you will get a good night's sleep.

Campers should move their camp every night so that their impacts are not concentrated in any one spot. Soils of the low deserts and scrub woodlands are particularly vulnerable to compaction. Compacted soils do not absorb water as well, and this leads to an increase in runoff. This in turn hastens soil erosion and leaves less water for desert plants, which may die as a result. By moving camp frequently, hikers will not compact the soil as severely, and the damage they do can be repaired by the activities of burrowing animals and insects. In addition, a human presence that is only temporary will be less likely to disturb behavior patterns of local wildlife.

There is something magical about having a campfire in the desert, with stars scattered across the infinite heavens like so much sparkling dust. Campfires can have major impacts on the desert community, however, and campers who build them should practice minimum-impact techniques so that their fire-building activities do not scar the landscape. To build a zero-impact fire, dig a pit 6 inches deep in mineral soil. Do not surround the pit with rocks; these will only get scorched and will not stop a fire from spreading in any case. Gather dead and downed twigs of small diameter (these will burn completely and leave no charred stumps). When your fire is spent, make sure the ash is cool to the touch, then bury it with the original soil. Scatter twigs sparsely across the site to camouflage it. Campfires are illegal in some areas, and firewood may be hard to find in others. Come prepared by bringing a lightweight backpacking stove in place of a campfire for all your cooking needs.

Finally, wilderness sanitation may be one of the next great problems facing land managers in southwestern Utah. Few outhouses are found in the Utah backcountry; thus, hikers must practice zero-impact techniques while having a bowel movement. When relieving yourself, select a site that is far from any stream, spring, or wash that might become contaminated. Dig a "cat hole" 4 to 6 inches deep in mineral soil, relieve yourself, and cover the site with soil. An even better solution is to carry a "poop tube" lined with paper bags to pack out any of your solid wastes. Such a tube can be constructed of a short length of PVC pipe, with screw-on caps at either end. This inexpensive, lightweight solution may represent the wave of the future in these arid lands.

For more information about zero-impact camping, visit the Leave No Trace website at LNT.org.

Flash Floods

In an area where soils are thin and bare rock covers much of the landscape, flash floods are an ever-present danger. Southwestern Utah is deeply scored with a network of spectacular chasms that bear mute testimony to the erosive power of the floodwaters. Floodwaters grow in magnitude rather than dispersing when they enter slot canyons, and any living thing that stands in the way of the water is sure to be swept away. Although no foolproof method can guarantee your safety in a narrow canyon, hikers can take three basic steps to reduce the chances of being caught in a flash flood.

First, assess the danger before you begin your trip. If rain threatens or a moisture-laden weather system is expected to pass through, do not venture into narrow canyons. Zion National Park uses the Flash Flood Warnings issued by the National Weather Service as a barometer to gauge risk and will close narrow canyon hikes during periods when a Flash Flood Warning is in effect. At other times, visitors are expected to check the weather forecast and make their own decisions regarding acceptable levels of risk.

The second step in avoiding death by flash flood is to continually reevaluate the potential for floods as you hike. Remember that a flood can occur under a clear blue sky if a downpour is in progress many miles away. Watch the skies for changing weather, and climb to safety or abort your hike if the clouds roll in. As you walk, watch the canyon walls for a muddy film and stranded driftwood that mark the high-water line during previous floods. Constantly scan the terrain for escape routes by which you can climb to safety above this high-water level. Also, keep your ears open. Flash floods make a muted roaring sound as they roll down a canyon, giving a few minutes' warning of the impending wall of water. An unaccountable roaring from upstream, often accompanied by a brisk and sudden wind, indicates the approach of floodwaters. Climb immediately to high ground.

The third step to surviving in a flood-prone environment is to know how to escape floodwaters if they overtake you. The best course of action is to climb out of harm's way, but the sheer walls found in many slot canyons often make it impossible to climb above the water. If you cannot escape by climbing, seek out a side cleft where you can hide from the full fury of the floodwaters. Large boulders can also be used as shelter from floods—wedge your body behind the lee side of the rock so that you will not be swept away by the initial surge. Remember that floating debris is as dangerous as the water itself; if you are knocked unconscious, you will certainly drown.

Also remember that a timely rescue is unlikely in the event of a backcountry flood. Be prepared to rescue yourself and your companions in an emergency. Carry a supply of extra food when hiking in backcountry canyons in case you are trapped for several days by floodwaters.

Planning Your Trip

Reading this guidebook to the Zion and Bryce region is a good start, but wise hikers will gather as much current information as possible before starting out on a wilderness expedition. Permits are not required for expeditions into most of Utah's public lands, although they are required for backpacking and some day hikes in the national parks. It is always wise to check in with a local ranger station to get the latest report on trail conditions. Ask for the trail supervisor or recreation planner, who will be well prepared to answer your questions. A list of addresses and phone numbers for these ranger stations is provided in Appendix B at the back of this book.

The key to a quality hiking experience is good planning. Hikers who underestimate the distance or time required to complete a trip may find themselves hiking in the dark, a dangerous proposition at best. Each hike is accompanied by an estimated hiking time, calculated using an average speed of 2 miles per hour. And note that these rates do not include stops for rest and refreshment, which add tremendously to a hiker's enjoyment and appreciation of the surroundings.

Eight miles a day is a good goal for travelers new to backpacking, while old hands can generally cover 10 miles comfortably. We recommend traveling below top speed, focusing more attention on the surrounding natural beauty and less on the exercise of hiking itself. In addition, desert heat and aridity make it unwise to push one's limits.

How to Use This Guide

The primary intent of this FalconGuide is to provide information that will help hikers choose trips according to their desires and abilities, as well as a detailed description of each trail, interpreting its natural and historical features. This guide is intended to be used in conjunction with topographic maps, which can be purchased at ranger stations and at local gift and sporting goods stores, or through the US Geological Survey, PO Box 25286, Federal Center, Denver, CO 80225. The USGS has stopped making the larger 15-minute map series and now publishes only 7.5-minute maps. Additionally, several fine topographic maps of larger areas have been published by various private organizations and are available in local stores.

In this book each trail description begins with an outline describing the physical characteristics of the trail. A general description of the trek comes first, followed by distance and the approximate hiking time. This description is followed by information on the best season for attempting the trail, which may be influenced by summer heat, winter snows, and/or wet season flooding.

Next is a difficulty rating. The rating can be interpreted as follows: Easy trails can be completed without difficulty by hikers of all abilities; hikes rated moderate will challenge novices; moderately strenuous hikes will tax even experienced hikers; and strenuous trails will push the physical limits of the most Herculean hiker.

Water availability along the trail is described next, according to its reliability. Even perennial, or year-round, water sources may dry up during drought years, and intermittent sources hold water only during the wet months. Wise hikers bring their own water rather than relying on natural supplies.

Next, for some hikes, are comments on trail hazards and recommended equipment to bring along. These are followed by the appropriate 7.5-minute quadrangle topo maps for each featured hike, which are listed in plain type. Maps published by sources other than the USGS appear in italics. The managing agency responsible for the area is then listed under jurisdiction, and a brief set of directions for finding the trailhead rounds out the statistical section.

A detailed interpretive description of the trail—including geologic and ecological features, historical sites, campsites, and other important information—follows.

The Miles and Directions at the end of some hikes provide a mile-by-mile description of landmarks, trail junctions, and gradient changes. The official distances of the land management agency are presented for all trails that had them at press time. Where official distances were unavailable, they were developed using an instrument called a planimeter, which measures two-dimensional distances on a topographic map. These distances were then corrected for altitude gain or loss. The resulting mileages should be looked upon as conservative estimates because they may not account for small-scale twists and turns or minor ups and downs.

Ranking the Hikes

From easiest to more challenging:

Map Legend

Symbol	Description
🛣 15	Interstate Highway
🛣 89	US Highway
🛣 9	State Highway
═══	County/Forest Road
───	Local Road
======	Gravel Road
------	Unimproved Road
▬▬▬▬	Featured Trail
- - - -	Trail
....	Off-Trail Route
～～	River/Creek
—··—··—	Intermittent Stream
⬭	Body of Water
≋	Marsh
▤	National Forest/Park/Wilderness
▤	State Park
▤	No Camping
✕	Airport
⌣	Bridge
■	Building/Point of Interest
▲	Campground
⨇	Cliff
•—•	Gate
⬛	Lodging
🅿	Parking
⌣	Pass/Gate
▲	Peak/Summit
🎋	Picnic Area
🏠	Ranger Station
⟋	Spring
○	Town
⑪	Trailhead
📷	Viewpoint/Overlook
❓	Visitor/Information Center
≋	Waterfall

Zion National Park and Surrounding Lands

Z ion National Park encompasses the landscape of high plateaus, deep canyons, and sheer monoliths surrounding the North Fork of the Virgin River. It is a relatively small park that receives heavy visitation, particularly the day-hiking trails within Zion Canyon. Although the trails in this guide are single-day hikes, some are point-to-point hikes requiring more than one car.

Access to Zion Canyon is via UT 9, about 22 miles east of Hurricane and 25 miles west of Mount Carmel Junction. The main park campground and visitor center are at the mouth of the canyon. A scenic spur road ascends the canyon to access trailheads and the Zion Park Lodge. Since this area receives heavy use, the National Park Service has closed the road to private vehicles and now provides access by free shuttles. Currently, private shuttles transport hikers to the upper trailhead for The Narrows.

Hikers can reach the plateaus east of the canyon by trail from the Zion Ponderosa Ranch Resort, on the gravel road to Navajo Lake. The western part of the Kolob Terrace is accessible via the paved Kolob Reservoir Road, which departs from the highway at the town of Virgin. A primitive campground and a fire lookout manned by rangers can be found atop Lava Point. At the western edge of the Kolob Terrace are the Kolob Canyons, surrounded by spectacular towers of stone. Access them by a paved road from I-15; a small visitor center here is permanently staffed by rangers.

The Zion Canyon Shuttle

The Park Service has instituted a shuttle service equipped with natural gas–powered trams to serve the popular Zion Canyon trailheads. The primary starting point for the tram is the main visitor center just east of Springdale, but during busy periods (when the visitor center parking lot is likely to be full), you can catch the tram at various marked points in the town of Springdale itself. There is no charge for the shuttle service, but riders are still required to pay the park entrance fee. The tram stops at Zion Canyon trailheads and points of interest four or more times each hour, from early morning to late evening. This shuttle service is fast and convenient, with plenty of room for backpacks.

1 East Mesa

A day hike offering access to Observation Point.

Distance: 3 miles (4.8 km) one way
Hiking time: About 1.5 hours
Best season: Apr–May, Sept–Nov
Difficulty: Easy
Water availability: None

Topo map: Temple of Sinawava; Zion National Park (Trails Illustrated)
Jurisdiction: Zion National Park. See Appendix B for more information.

Finding the trailhead: From Zion National Park's East Entrance, drive east on UT 9 for 2.4 miles to a junction with a paved road that runs north toward Navajo Lake and The Narrows trailhead. Turn left onto this paved road, and after 5.3 miles it arrives at the Zion Ponderosa Ranch Resort. Don't forget to sign in and out of the book in the mailbox at the gate. Pass through the main entrance and drive west on the main route, which is Twin Knolls Road. The road ends at a T intersection; turn right and follow Beaver Road northward. This road deteriorates into a primitive track, which ultimately swings west to enter Zion National Park at the beginning of the East Mesa Trail. GPS: N37° 17' 42.229" / W112° 54' 1.734"

The Hike

This trail provides a shorter and easier route to Observation Point and, in contrast to the paved trail from Weeping Rock, is open to horses. The path begins by running west from the national park boundary through an open stand of ponderosa pine. This country burned in patches during 1995, clearing much of the underbrush. Lightning strikes are common atop the high plateaus of Zion, and the plant community found here is well adapted to periodic burns. Ponderosa pines have

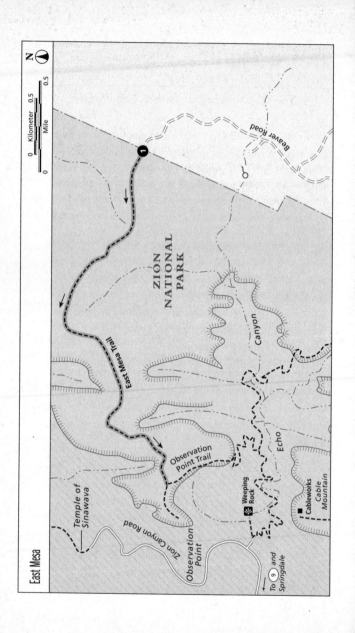

East Mesa

ZION NATIONAL PARK

East Mesa Trail

Observation Point Trail

Temple of Sinawava

Zion Canyon Road

Observation Point

Weeping Rock

Echo Canyon

Cableworks

Cable Mountain

To 9 and Springdale

Beaver Road

N

0   Kilometer   0.5

0   Mile   0.5

1

thick bark that protects them from the flames, and their seedlings do well in the sunny openings created by fires. Manzanita is a fire-adapted shrub that benefits from periodic burns by colonizing the new openings in the forest.

The first views of the hike are northward, and they feature the lofty Pink Cliffs of the Virgin Rim, which rise to 10,000 feet along the northern horizon. These cliffs are made up of freshwater limestone that is colored by oxides of iron and manganese. Below them is the Gray Cliffs band, an older layer made of shale deposited in a marine environment.

After 1.5 miles the trail approaches a low knoll. Side paths diverging to the right are bound for overlooks of Mystery Canyon. The White Cliffs found in this canyon are of the same Navajo sandstone that makes up the walls of Zion Canyon. This formation, even more ancient than the marine shales of the Gray Cliffs, was laid down as windblown sand dunes during the Jurassic Period.

The main trail soon swings southwest, revealing views of Echo Canyon as well as the lower reaches of Zion Canyon itself. The West Temple rises prominently above its rim, capped with a thin band of reddish limestone. The trail strikes the south rim of a nameless cleft that joins the Virgin River just below The Narrows, offering excellent views of the White Cliffs. Upon crossing a low saddle, the trail passes several sandy camp spots and then makes a brief descent to meet the Observation Point Trail 0.2 mile from its terminus.

Key Points

0.0   East Mesa trailhead.

3.0   Trail ends at junction with Observation Point Trail.

2 Canyon Overlook

A short out-and-back day hike to an overlook of lower Zion Canyon.

Distance: 1 mile (1.6 km) out-and-back
Hiking time: About 0.5 hour
Best season: Mar–Nov
Difficulty: Moderate
Water availability: None
Hazards: Cliff exposure

Topo maps: Springdale East; Zion National Park (Trails Illustrated)
Jurisdiction: Zion National Park. See Appendix B for more information.

Finding the trailhead: From the Zion Visitor Center, drive east on UT 9 for 5 miles. The trailhead is just beyond the first tunnel. GPS: N37° 12' 44.163" / W112° 56' 24.753"

The Hike

This short but scenic trail runs to a high overlook immediately above the Great Arch, commanding vistas of the lower reaches of Zion Canyon. Interpretive brochures found at the trailhead explain the plants, animals, and geological features found along the route.

The path initially climbs a series of stairsteps and then traverses across the upper walls of the deep slot canyon of Pine Creek. The path passes beneath several overhangs and in a few spots offers uneven footing above dropoffs; proceed with caution. The path ultimately emerges onto a hilltop covered with hoodoos, or pillars of eroded stone. It then weaves across the slickrock and between piñon pines to reach Canyon Overlook, a spectacular vista point. East

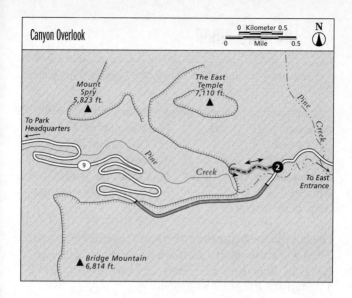

Temple looms to the north, while to the west spreads a panorama highlighted by Bridge Mountain, the West Temple, the Towers of the Virgin, and the Streaked Wall. Travelers carrying binoculars can glass the cliffs to the south for desert bighorn sheep, which have been reintroduced into Zion National Park.

Key Points

- **0.0** Trailhead on UT 9.
- **0.5** Canyon Overlook.
- **1.0** Arrive back at the trailhead.

3 The Watchman

An out-and-back hike into the foothills below The Watchman and Bridge Mountain.

Distance: 2 miles (3.2 km) out-and-back
Hiking time: About 1 hour
Best season: Apr-Oct
Difficulty: Easy
Water availability: None

Topo maps: Springdale East; Zion National Park (Trails Illustrated)
Jurisdiction: Zion National Park. See Appendix B for more information.

Finding the trailhead: Head north from Zion National Park's South Entrance and take the first right toward The Watchman Campground. Park in the visitor center lot and walk to the trailhead. GPS: N37° 11' 54.812" / W112° 59' 12.826"

The Hike

Climbing into the foothills beneath Bridge Mountain and The Watchman, this short trail begins from the shuttle stop and follows the bank of the Virgin River upstream. After crossing a service road, a set of wooden steps leads northward up a small knoll. Stay on the main trail, avoiding side trails created by a large population of mule deer. The official trail is about 3 feet wide and traverses the base of the first knoll toward the National Park Service residential areas. The vegetation in this area is characterized by a scrub woodland of juniper and piñon pine with sagebrush in the sunny openings.

The path then turns east and proceeds up the base of Bridge Mountain via a series of long switchbacks. Hikers will view overhanging cliffs and stratified rock layers along

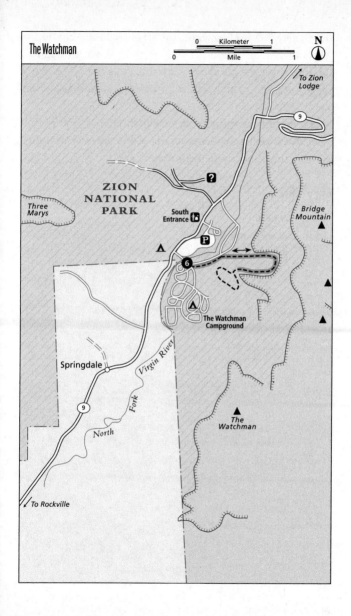

The Watchman

ZION
NATIONAL
PARK

Three
Marys

To Zion
Lodge

9

Bridge
Mountain

South
Entrance

The Watchman
Campground

Springdale

Virgin River

North Fork

The
Watchman

To Rockville

N

Kilometer 1

Mile 1

the trail as they ascend across the stone walls. In addition to views of Bridge Mountain and The Watchman throughout the hike, travelers can look westward across the Virgin River for a fine vista of the Towers of the Virgin, and also south toward the town of Springdale.

At the top of this trail, a loop path crowns the foothill. This short loop provides several good perches from which to view surrounding geological wonders.

Key Points

0.0 Trailhead.

1.0 The Watchman viewpoint.

2.0 Arrive back at the trailhead.

4 West Bank of the Virgin River

A day hike along the Virgin River, from the Court of the Patriarchs viewpoint to the Grotto trailhead.

Distance: 2.6 miles (4.2 km) one way
Hiking time: About 1.25 hours
Best season: Year-round
Difficulty: Easy
Water availability: The Virgin River always has water, but it is silty.

Topo maps: Springdale East, Temple of Sinawava; Zion National Park (Trails Illustrated)
Jurisdiction: Zion National Park. See Appendix B for more information.

Finding the trailhead: The trail begins at the Court of the Patriarchs viewpoint, 2.2 miles up Zion Canyon Road (take the tram). It ends at the Grotto trailhead, at mile 3.2 on Zion Canyon Road. GPS of start: N37° 14' 6.854" / W112° 57' 46.124"; GPS of finish: N37° 15' 28.592" / W112° 56' 58.601"

The Hike

Following trails along the west bank of the Virgin River, this short hike provides an alternative to the scenic drive for visitors who prefer to experience nature outside their cars. The trail is level and easy, but it is heavily traveled by horse parties between the Emerald Pools trailhead and the Court of the Patriarchs. Nonstop views of Zion Canyon are found all along the route, and the lowlands along the river are excellent places to spot birds and, in twilight hours, mule deer.

From the Court of the Patriarchs viewpoint, follow the service road west past a large water tank to reach a bridge over the Virgin River. After crossing the bridge, turn left and follow the trail into the center of the Court of the Patriarchs. Views are stunning beneath the giant monoliths of Navajo sandstone that line this deep alcove in the wall of Zion Canyon.

Continuing on, hikers will reach an unmarked trail junction at the edge of a grassy hill; turn right as the path climbs to an arid knoll and passes the remains of an old corral. The trail levels off here and follows the river northward. Due to the gradient of the river, hikers will reach the river bottoms without any noticeable loss of altitude. The bottomlands are robed in a riparian woodland of cottonwood and box elder. Mule deer often appear on the far bank of the river during the twilight hours. This is also the habitat of the elusive ring-tailed cat, which hides beneath rock overhangs by day and ventures forth to forage at night.

The trail follows the river upward as the bleached summits of Mount Majestic and Cathedral Mountain rise beyond the reddish spire called The Spearhead. After a corral across the river marks an end to the horse traffic, a bridge spans the river, allowing hikers access to the Emerald Pools trailhead. The trail now becomes wide and paved. Foot traffic is heavy as the route climbs steadily before dipping into the stone amphitheater that bears the Emerald Pools. Spur trails climb to the upper pools, while the main trail runs around the edge of Lower Emerald Pool, with its rock overhang, delicate waterfalls, and hanging gardens. Bear right and follow signs for the Grotto trailhead as the trail threads its way through these picturesque rock gardens to reach a fine viewpoint at the bowl's edge.

The path then traverses northward, staying above a low cliff of Springdale sandstone, which is older than the Navajo Formation that overtops it. The Great White Throne presents its alabaster profile above the far bank of the river as the trail covers the final distance to a bridge that leads to the Grotto trailhead.

Key Points

0.0 Court of the Patriarchs viewpoint. Follow service road to river.

0.1 Footbridge over the North Fork of the Virgin River

0.3 Trail junction. Turn right for West Bank Trail.

1.3 Horse ford to corrals on east bank of river. Trail to Middle and Upper Emerald pools climbs to left. Keep going straight.

1.4 Footbridge with access to Zion Lodge.

1.9 Lower Emerald Pool.

2.0 Junction with trail to upper pools. Bear right.

2.6 Junction with Angels Landing/West Rim Trail. Cross bridge to finish the hike at the Grotto trailhead.

5 Emerald Pools

A network of trails of varied lengths to the Lower, Middle, and/or Upper Emerald Pools.

Distance: 1.9-mile (3 km) loop with options
Hiking time: About 1 hour
Best season: Mar–Nov
Difficulty: Easy (Lower Pool); moderate (Upper Pool)
Water availability: Emerald Pools have a permanent supply of water, but hikers are asked to bring their own drinking water.
Topo maps: Temple of Sinawava, Zion National Park (Trails Illustrated)
Jurisdiction: Zion National Park. See Appendix B for more information.

Finding the trailhead: From the Zion Visitor Center, take the Zion Canyon tram to Zion Lodge. The trailhead and parking area are on the west side of the road opposite the lodge. GPS: N37° 14' 58.265" / W112° 57' 27.448"

The Hike

There are three Emerald Pools—Upper, Middle, and Lower—and visitors may choose from as many trails: a short, 1.2-mile round-trip loop to the Lower Pool; a 2-mile round-trip visit to the Middle and Lower Pools; or a 2.5-mile round-trip hike to all three. The paths to the Lower and Middle Pools are wide sidewalks and easily traveled. The Lower Pool is accessible to people in wheelchairs if they have assistance. The trail from the Middle Pool to the Upper Pool is more difficult. This path is no longer maintained and is classified by the National Park Service as strenuous, with its uneven sand and rock surface and moderate to strenuous grade.

While visiting these pools bear in mind that the National Park Service has spent considerable funds to restore and protect these pools. Contribute to this effort by refraining from bathing in or walking through the water.

From the parking area cross the bridge to the west side of the Virgin River, where a trailhead sign is located. Hikers who wish to travel directly to the Lower Pool can take the sidewalk to the right. The Middle Pool Trail is no longer a trail, but the Middle Pool can still be reached via Lower Pool Trail or Kayenta Trail. Those wishing to visit the Middle and Upper Pools should follow the path that climbs to the left. The trail description here follows the rocky path that climbs toward the Middle and Upper Pools.

The trail briefly parallels the Virgin River. Portions of the path have been paved with concrete. The trail up to the Middle Pool is lined with box elder, juniper, bigtooth maple, and Gambel oak. As it progresses up the slope, the trail presents views of formations such as Lady Mountain, the Spearhead, Mount Majestic, Red Arch Mountain, Deertrap Mountain, and the Great White Throne rising above Zion Canyon.

The Middle Pool occupies a large, open area surrounded by slickrock. Pools of water have collected from the trickles above. At the edge of the main pool is a long drop-off leading down to Lower Emerald Pool. From this vantage point visitors can look out over canyon bottoms filled with a lush deciduous forest.

Traverse across the Middle Pool area to find a small trailhead sign that marks a narrow path to the Upper Pool. This short, 0.3-mile trail is no longer maintained by the park staff. The trail is uneven and rocky and climbs up a moderately strenuous grade. The Upper Pool itself is surrounded on

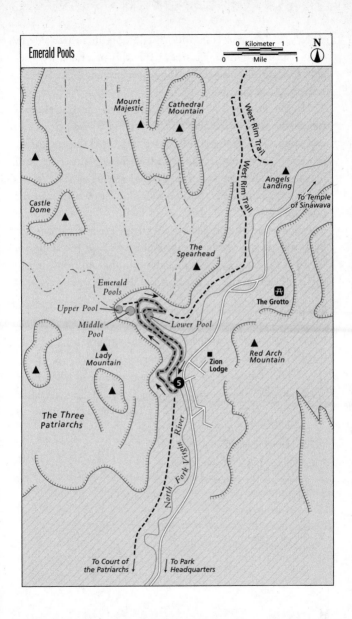

three sides by sheer cliffs and closed in on the fourth side by a boulder foothill. Maple trees shade this natural amphitheater, making this one of the most peaceful day-hike destinations in Zion Canyon.

To get from the Middle Pool down to the Lower Pool, follow the well-worn path to the north. This trail turns east and splits: The higher trail runs toward the Grotto Picnic Area, while the lower path heads to Lower Emerald Pool. The trail to Lower Emerald Pool descends quickly along stone steps peppered with sand. Looking down toward the pool, visitors will see a large alcove with a fine veil of water dripping over its edge and into a large mirror surrounded by Gambel oak, maple, and box elder. Follow the trail as it winds beneath the alcove past the pool before returning to the trailhead on the far bank of the Virgin River.

Key Points

0.0 Trailhead for Lower Pool. Turn left to begin loop trip.

0.9 Middle Emerald Pool; junction with trail to Upper Emerald Pool (*Option:* This 0.3 mile trail is moderately strenuous.)

1.2 Junction with trail to Lower Emerald Pool and trail to Grotto Picnic Area. Turn right to visit the Lower Pool and return to trailhead.

1.3 Lower Emerald Pool.

1.9 Arrive back at the trailhead.

6 Angels Landing

An out-and-back day hike to the summit of Angels Landing.

Distance: 5.4 miles (8.7 km) out-and-back
Hiking time: About 2 hours
Best season: Mar–Nov
Difficulty: Strenuous
Water availability: The Virgin River always has water, but it is silty.

Hazards: Cliff exposure
Topo maps: Temple of Sinawava; Zion National Park (Trails Illustrated)
Jurisdiction: Zion National Park. See Appendix B for more information.

Finding the trailhead: The trail begins at the Grotto trailhead, 0.6 mile beyond Zion Lodge on Zion Canyon Road (accessed via the tram). GPS: N37° 15' 28.592" / W112° 56' 58.601" W

The Hike

This trail provides a spectacular day trip for well-conditioned hikers who have no fear of heights. It receives heavy use, so chances for solitude are slim. Beyond Scout Lookout, the trail becomes an uneven route across sheer cliffs, with chains bolted into the rock face to serve as handrails. This part of the route can be extremely slippery and dangerous when wet or icy and should be avoided unless dry conditions can be depended upon. It is not a good place to take young children in any weather.

The trail begins by crossing a bridge over the Virgin River and then turns north at a junction with the Kayenta Trail. Following the river, the path passes through a riparian woodland of cottonwood and box elder, with canyon grape and tamarisk growing in the understory. Tamarisk was originally brought to the Southwest as an ornamental plant, but it soon escaped from cultivated areas and now crowds out native shrubs in many desert wash environments. Angels Landing looms ahead, with the mouth of Refrigerator Canyon tucked between this monolith and the west wall of Zion Canyon.

The trail climbs vigorously to reach the elevated mouth of Refrigerator Canyon and then levels off as it enters the cool inner recesses of the cleft. Cool-climate plants such as bigtooth maple and white fir thrive in the shade of the canyon floor, and the vertical walls of red sandstone are pocked with grottos and overhangs.

As the path nears the head of the canyon, it begins a strenuous ascent of the east wall. A series of twenty-one switchbacks has been built cunningly into a rift in the wall here and bears the traveler upward at a calf-burning pace. Known as "Walter's Wiggles," these carefully crafted stoneworks are regarded as one of the engineering marvels of the park. Soon after reaching the top of the switchbacks, the path makes a gradual ascent to a sandy pad called Scout Lookout. It occupies the saddle behind Angels Landing, offering aerial views into Zion Canyon for travelers who lack the stomach for the final and hair-raising pitch to the top of Angels Landing.

The West Rim Trail climbs northwest from Scout Lookout, while the Angels Landing Trail bears southeast. It follows the spine of a knife-edge ridge, with heavy chains attached to the rock to serve as handrails along most (but not all) of the drop-offs. Hikers must make a steep scramble to surmount the first knob, followed by an unprotected walk across a narrow saddle that is flanked by sheer drop-offs. One truly gets

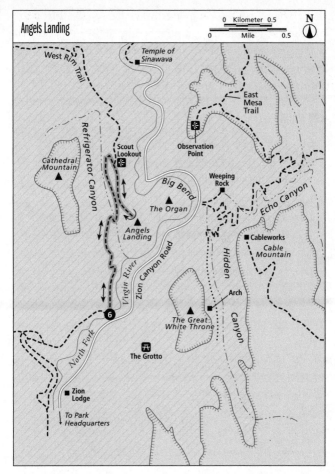

0   Kilometer   0.5

0   Mile   0.5

N

West Rim Trail

Temple of Sinawava

East Mesa Trail

Refrigerator Canyon

Cathedral Mountain ▲

Scout Lookout

Observation Point

Big Bend

Weeping Rock

Echo Canyon

The Organ

Angels Landing

Zion Canyon Road

Cableworks

Cable Mountain

Virgin River

Hidden Canyon

6

North Fork

Arch

The Great White Throne ▲

The Grotto

Zion Lodge

To Park Headquarters

a feeling of walking on the razor's edge here. Climbing then resumes, aided by more handrails and footholds hewn into bedrock. This is the long and final pitch to the summit.

There are no guardrails on Angels Landing, where gnarled piñon pines grow from impossible toeholds above the dizzying void. Occupying the center of the Big Bend of Zion Canyon, the summit commands a spectacular 360-degree panorama of rugged spires and towering walls. Highlights include the Great White Throne, Red Arch Mountain, and the entrance to The Narrows.

Key Points

0.0 The Grotto trailhead

0.1 Footbridge over North Fork of Virgin River and junction with West Bank trail. Turn right for Angels Landing.

1.1 Trail enters Refrigerator Canyon.

1.8 Junction with West Rim Trail at Scout Lookout. Turn right for summit of Angels Landing. Footing becomes treacherous.

2.2 Angels Landing summit.

4.4 Arrive back at the trailhead.

7 Sand Bench Loop

A loop day hike through arid uplands in lower Zion Canyon.

Distance: 7.6-mile (12.2 km) loop
Hiking time: About 2 hours
Best season: Sept–May
Difficulty: Moderate
Water availability: The Virgin River always has water, but it is silty.

Recommended equipment: Gaiters
Topo maps: Springdale East; Zion National Park (Trails Illustrated)
Jurisdiction: Zion National Park. See Appendix B for more information.

Finding the trailhead: Take the Zion Canyon tram to Court of the Patriarchs viewpoint, 2.2 miles up Zion Canyon Road. The hike starts from the viewpoint. GPS: N37° 14' 6.854" / W112° 57' 46.124"

The Hike

This sandy trail loops onto an elevated bench on the far side of the Virgin River, visiting the Court of the Patriarchs and the Streaked Wall along the way. It is heavily used by park concessionaires for horse tours, so hikers should be prepared to share the trail with heavy horse traffic during the peak season (April through October). For this reason rangers do not recommend the trail as a hiking route.

From the Court of the Patriarchs viewpoint, walk westward down the service road and past a large water tank to reach a footbridge over the river. Turn left on the far bank. The trail wanders up into the sagebrush meadows in the center of the Court of the Patriarchs. Immense monoliths

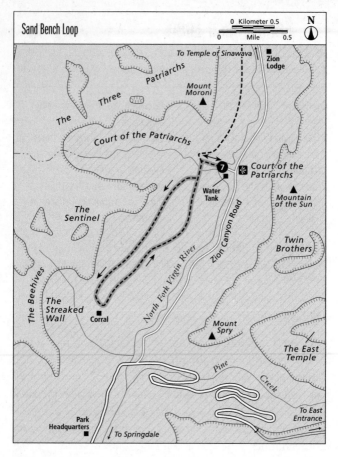

Sand Bench Loop

0 Kilometer 0.5
0 Mile 0.5

N

To Temple of Sinawava

Zion Lodge

Patriarchs

Mount Moroni

Three

The

Court of the Patriarchs

7 Court of the Patriarchs

Water Tank

Mountain of the Sun

The Sentinel

Zion Canyon Road

Twin Brothers

North Fork Virgin River

The Beehives

The Streaked Wall

Corral

Mount Spry

The East Temple

Pine Creek

Park Headquarters

To East Entrance

To Springdale

of ancient stone rise on all sides, giving visitors a humbling perspective on their own significance. There is another junction here; turn left and cross a small streambed to begin the Sand Bench Loop.

The trail then begins a steady climb and soon splits to form the loop. This description follows the right fork first, but the loop can be hiked in either direction with equal ease. As it climbs, the west fork of the trail passes beneath the foot of sheer walls and rugged towers.

The trail tops out on a sandy alluvial fan populated by deep-rooted sagebrush. The Streaked Wall looms ahead on the near side of the canyon, while the ragged walls of the Watchman are visible farther down the valley. The trail then glides down onto a flat bench at the foot of the Streaked Wall, where tilted rocks rise among the piñon pines and juniper. A rest area and corral mark the southern end of the loop.

From here the trail runs northward, skirting the edge of an escarpment high above the river. Superb views of the East Temple, the Twin Brothers, and the Mountain of the Sun accompany hikers for the remainder of the trek.

Key Points

0.0 Court of the Patriarchs viewpoint. Follow service road to river.

0.1 Footbridge over North Fork of the Virgin River.

0.3 Trail junction. Turn left for Sand Bench Loop.

0.9 Sand Bench Loop splits. Take right fork.

2.5 Trails rejoin to complete the loop.

3.4 Arrive back at Court of the Patriarchs viewpoint.

8 Eagle Crags

An out-and-back climb to the foot of Eagle Crags in the Vermilion Cliffs.

Distance: 6.2 miles (9.6 km) out-and-back
Hiking time: About 3 hours
Best season: Mar–May, Sept–Nov
Difficulty: Moderately strenuous
Water availability: None
Hazards: Unstable footing on steep, rocky slopes

Topo maps: Springdale West, Smithsonian Butte; Zion National Park (Trails Illustrated)
Jurisdiction: Bureau of Land Management, St. George Field Office. See Appendix B for more information.

Finding the trailhead: From the South Entrance of Zion National Park, drive 4.7 miles west on UT 9 to Rockville. Head south (left) on Grafton Road and go 0.3 mile to Bridge Road, an unimproved road. Bridge Road has an uneven surface and traverses up steep slopes with few places to turn around. A high-clearance vehicle is recommended from this point on. Several private residences are located at the top of the hill. When the road splits into three branches, continue up the middle road. After 1.4 miles look for a trailhead sign and pullout area on the right. GPS: N37° 8' 40.740" / W113° 1' 48.447"

The Hike

This is a moderately strenuous hike into the Mount Canaan Wilderness with both gradual and steep changes in elevation. The trail surface is uneven and rocky in most areas, with the exception of some areas east and south of the crags, which are predominantly sand. The trail itself travels across land managed by the Bureau of Land Management to reach the foot of Eagle Crags, a series of knifelike pinnacles rising from a lone butte. It then climbs a series of switchbacks to provide closer views of the towering spires.

From the trailhead follow the path to the right of the trailhead sign, and head down a slope to the south. The trail is predominantly sandy, rocky, and uneven and is used heavily by horse parties. If you encounter horses on the trail, step aside and yield the right-of-way. Early on the trail, hikers can see the Eagle Crags to the south and Shunesburg Mountain to the east.

The trail continues downhill until it crosses a draw and ascends the opposite foothill on a southeasterly heading. During this ascent visitors will encounter a hiker gate through a barbed-wire fence. Pass through the gate and continue to climb southeast across the foothills of the Crags. Along the way are eastward views of the Vermilion Cliffs and South Mountain.

After eventually turning down into a draw and traversing another wash, the path turns east and parallels the wash as it makes its way around the base of the foothill to the right (south). The trail then approaches a confluence and turns south, staying on the west side and paralleling the contributing wash. The trail crosses the wash and continues southeast.

Views of Eagle Crags are sometimes hidden by the foothills as the trail winds around to the northeast side of the formation. The trail soon emerges onto an open slope, however, and begins to ascend below the east side of the crags. This slope offers uninterrupted views of Shunesburg Mountain, the Vermilion Cliffs, and South Creek.

At the top of the slope, the trail turns right and heads up to the crags via a series of switchbacks. This is a moderate climb over an uneven, rocky path. At the foot of the crags, the trail straightens out and briefly levels off. The quite narrow

Eagle Crags

0 Kilometer 0.5

0 Mile 0.5

N

To Bridge Road
& ⑨

Eagle Crags ▲

⑧

path then begins to climb across a steep slope—watch your footing. At the end of this slope, the trail passes a large, flat, overhanging rock from which junipers are growing. After more climbing, hikers reach the crest of the foothill and the eastern end of the crag formations.

Looking up at the spires, travelers will see the reason for the name Eagle Crags. Enjoy the fine views across the valley to the east before you head back along the same route from this great turnaround spot.

Hikers can follow the upward path a short distance to its very end as it wraps around to the south side of the crags. Staying in the upland areas, the route passes over two draws. The path across the draws is narrow and uneven with loose rocks and steep slopes. Use careful footing along this stretch. Beyond the draws the path gradually loses elevation. As it heads down toward the head of South Creek, the trail abruptly ends in a series of small runoff washes. Another path leads down a very steep slope into a large draw, but it ends abruptly on the other side.

Key Points

- **0.0**   Start at the BLM trailhead sign.
- **3.1**   Trail ends below Eagle Crags.
- **6.2**   Arrive back at the trailhead.

9 Northgate Peaks

A short day hike to an overlook between the Northgate Peaks.

Distance: 2.2 miles (3.5 km) one way

Hiking time: About 1 hour

Best season: May–Oct

Difficulty: Easy

Water availability: A seep east of Pocket Mesa is intermittent.

Topo map: Zion National Park (Trails Illustrated)

Jurisdiction: Zion National Park. See Appendix B for more information.

Finding the trailhead: From the town of Virgin, follow the paved Kolob Reservoir Road northward. The road crosses the boundary of Zion National Park three times on its way to the Wildcat Canyon trailhead at mile 16. The hike begins here. GPS: N38° 57' 34.749" / W113° 7' 14.594"

The Hike

This trail offers an easy day trip with fine scenery, but it receives relatively little use because of its location in a remote corner of the park. The trek begins in the shadow of Pine Valley Peak, a lone pinnacle of bone-white Navajo sandstone. The path heads eastward across open sage meadows; soon a sprinkling of pines rises to either side. Upon approaching the compact mass of Pocket Mesa, the path veers southward and the pines coalesce into a gladed woodland.

In the midst of the savannah, the trail reaches a junction with the Wildcat Canyon and Connector Trails; turn left here. After an eastward jog of 0.1 mile, you'll see a signpost marking the spot where the Northgate Peaks Trail breaks away to the south. Turn right and follow the path to the top of a rise, where a well-beaten spur splits to the left en route to an overlook of the white cliffs of Russell Gulch and onward into the canyon of the Left Fork. The main trail continues straight ahead, following the crest of a promontory that is cloaked in copses of pine and grassy meadows. This path runs out onto a lava outcrop presenting a spectacular view of the Northgate Peaks and North Guardian Angel.

Key Points

- **0.0** Wildcat Canyon trailhead.
- **0.9** Junction with Wildcat Canyon and Connector Trails. Turn left.
- **1.0** Junction with Northgate Peaks Trail. Turn right (south).
- **2.2** Northgate Peaks overlook.

10 Middle Fork of Taylor Creek

A trail along the Middle Fork of Taylor Creek, ending at Double Arch Alcove.

Distance: 2.5 miles (4 km) one way
Hiking time: About 1 hour
Best season: Mar–Nov
Difficulty: Easy
Water availability: Reliable

Topo maps: Kolob Arch; Zion National Park (Trails Illustrated)
Jurisdiction: Zion National Park. See Appendix B for more information.

Finding the trailhead: Follow I-15 to the Kolob Canyons Visitor Center. From the visitor center drive 2 miles east along the park road to a parking area on the left (north) side of the road. Look for the trailhead sign on the east side of the parking lot. GPS: N37° 27' 39.434" / W113° 11' 52.191"

The Hike

This easy trail takes hikers up the canyon of the Middle Fork of Taylor Creek to two historic homestead cabins and Double Arch Alcove. An alcove is a "blind" arch formed in a rock face through which there are no gaps for daylight to pass. In addition to Double Arch Alcove, hikers are rewarded with spectacular views of Tucupit Point and Paria Point as they approach the canyon. The creek bed is fairly narrow, so be prepared to get wet at numerous stream crossings, and it can be chilly in early spring.

The trail begins from a sign at the east end of the parking lot. The path immediately descends a set of wooden steps down to the creek bed. The vegetation bordering the creek consists of manzanita, sagebrush, juniper, ponderosa pine, and piñon pine. From the bottom of the staircase, the path turns right and heads upstream toward the mouth of the canyon, with views of Horse Ranch Mountain off to the left (northeast). Portions of the trail are sandy and may offer difficult traveling after rains.

The path is easy to follow as it crisscrosses the watercourse several times. Beyond the sixth crossing hikers may confuse the path with other social trails in the area. The main trail departs from the north bank of the stream, crosses a small island and then picks up again on the south bank. As streamside benches begin to narrow, travel along the trail becomes a bit more difficult. The trail climbs up and out of the stream bottoms several times.

After a mile the trail reaches the confluence of the North and Middle Forks. Look for a trail sign and the Larson homestead cabin in this area. Gustav Larson built the cabin in 1930 from white fir logs hauled in by wagon from Cedar City. He spent summers here from 1930 to 1933, homesteading the Kolob area and raising pigs.

Beyond the cabin the trail crosses the North Fork and ascends into the canyon between Tucupit and Paria Points. Once inside the canyon, the trail stays low along the creek bed. A second homestead cabin can be found about three-quarters of the way up the canyon on a bench above the north bank of the creek. Arthur Fife built this cabin from white fir logs in 1930. Fife was a teacher at Southern Utah State College, now Southern Utah University. When not teaching, he spent his time at the cabin raising goats.

As hikers near the end of the trail, the path climbs onto the south bench to bypass a fallen tree lying in the creek bed.

Middle Fork of Taylor Creek

The trail ends at Double Arch Alcove, with its spectacular streaked overhang that encloses a shady pocket.

Key Points

0.0 Start at the trailhead.

1.0 Confluence of North and Middle Forks of Taylor Creek.

2.5 Trail ends at Double Arch Alcove.

Cedar Breaks and Markagunt High Country

The Markagunt Plateau is one of the loftiest uplands in western Utah. The Paiute gave the plateau its name, which means "Highland of Trees." Indeed, a rich forest of subalpine fir and spruce graces the rolling surface of the plateau, interspersed with broad, grassy meadows where elk and mule deer come to graze. Bristlecone pines cling to the windy precipices on the rims of the plateau, surviving extremes of cold and drought.

Because of the plateau's high elevation, hiking opportunities are limited to the summer months. The deep snowdrifts of winter often linger until June, and autumn snows force road closures as early as October. Cool summer temperatures atop the Markagunt make it a haven from the scorching heat found at lower elevations. In winter the area receives enough snow for cross-country skiing. Access to the Markagunt Plateau is via Utah Highway 14, which runs between Cedar City and Long Valley Junction. The highway is plowed free of snow during the wintertime, but only during daylight hours.

The jewel in the crown of the Markagunt Plateau is Cedar Breaks National Monument. This small preserve encompasses a broad amphitheater filled with cliffs banded in orange and red, castellated with craggy spires and natural arches that rival Bryce Canyon in splendor.

11 Spectra Point–Ramparts Trail

A short, out-and-back day hike along the rim of the Cedar Breaks.

Distance: 4 miles (6.5 km) out-and-back
Hiking time: About 1.5 to 2 hours
Best season: June–Sept
Difficulty: Moderately strenuous due to elevation gain and loss
Water availability: The small stream to the west of Spectra Point flows permanently.

Hazards: Cliff exposure, lightning
Topo map: Cedar Breaks National Monument
Jurisdiction: Cedar Breaks National Monument. See Appendix B for more information.

Finding the trailhead: From Cedar City drive east on UT 14 for 17.9 miles, then turn north on UT 148. Follow this road for 3 miles to reach the Cedar Breaks Visitor Center. The Ramparts Trail departs from the west end of the visitor center parking lot. GPS: N37° 36' 41.452" / W112° 50' 11.246"

The Hike

This trail follows the south rim of the Cedar Breaks amphitheater, revealing sweeping vistas of the ragged walls and eroded pinnacles that fill the basin. From the parking lot the path ascends for a short distance to the cliff tops above Jericho Canyon. Here it skirts among wind-scoured stands of Englemann spruce and subalpine fir. Some of these trees have been tortured by windblown snow to such an extent that they have taken on the dwarfed krumm-holz growth form. This low, matlike growth results when windblown crystals of ice prune off the buds that protrude above the snowdrifts.

Views are spectacular from the outset of the hike, featuring multicolored spires and fins of weathered limestone. The bands of red, orange, and even lavender are derived from the oxidation of iron and manganese, which were deposited when the rock-forming sediments here were laid down at the bottom of an enormous freshwater lake. As the trail winds in and out of the trees, hikers get southward views of the meadowy top of the Markagunt Plateau.

After a mile a spur path runs out to the end of Spectra Point. This long finger of chalky limestone extends northward into the heart of the Cedar Breaks amphitheater. It is one of the finest vantage points for viewing the area's hoodoos and walls, especially during morning and evening, when slanting light illuminates the stone. Prominent features of the badlands include Bristlecone and Chessmen Ridges, which rise from the center of the amphitheater, castellated with tortured pinnacles of all descriptions.

Growing from the arid soils of Spectra Point are hardy specimens of bristlecone pine, twisted by winter gales and splintered by summer lightning storms. The oldest specimen on the point is more than 1,600 years old; the longest-lived bristlecone, located in California, has survived for more than 4,500 years.

The main trail departs westward from Spectra Point, zigzagging downward into a wooded glen occupied by a crystal-clear rivulet. Spruce, fir, and limber pine tower overhead, shading luxuriant swards of grasses and wildflowers that include lupine, aster, bluebells, and larkspur. The trail descends at a steady clip, making occasional forays to the rims for views of the badlands that stretch away below.

Spectra Point–Ramparts Trail

The trail ends at a high overlook of the Rampart, which bears a scattered growth of bristlecone pine. From this point views stretch from the forested floor of the basin all the way to the banded cliffs that rise 2,000 feet all around it.

Key Points

0.0 Trail leaves parking lot.

1.0 Spectra Point.

2.0 Trail peters out atop the Rampart. Turn around and retrace your steps.

4.0 Arrive back at the parking lot.

12 Alpine Pond

A short loop trail through wooded country atop the Markagunt Plateau.

Distance: 2.1-mile (3.4 km)
loop
Hiking time: About 1 hour
Best season: June–Sept
Difficulty: Moderate
Water availability: Alpine Pond
always has water but is ecologi-
cally fragile; take water only from

the outlet stream below the
pond.
Topo map: Cedar Breaks
National Monument
Jurisdiction: Cedar Breaks
National Monument. See Appen-
dix B for more information.

Finding the trailhead: The trail departs from the Chessmen Overlook, 1.7 miles beyond the Cedar Breaks Visitor Center on UT 148.
The trail can also be accessed from the Alpine Pond trailhead, 1 mile
farther north. GPS: N37° 37' 53.113" / W112° 49' 53.020"

The Hike

This trail forms a loop through the subalpine forest above
the east rim of the Cedar Breaks amphitheater. It is a self-
guiding nature walk, with pamphlets provided at either
trailhead. We describe the trek as a 2.1-mile loop from the
Chessmen Overlook, but hikers can also approach the loop
from the Alpine Pond trailhead at its north end or choose
between several shorter point-to-point hikes.

From the overlook follow the Lower Trail downward
through a forest of stately spruce and fir. A handful of bristlecone pines grow along the rim of the amphitheater, and gaps
in the trees allow glimpses of the northern half of the Cedar

Breaks. Less rugged than the southern reaches, the cliffs and spires that appear here are sprinkled with a sparse growth of conifers. The trail follows the rim for almost a mile and then enters a wooded dale that bears the headwaters of Rattle Creek.

The path climbs to the source of the waters, a tiny spring-fed lake known as Alpine Pond. This crystal-clear pool is cupped within a miniature basin surrounded by elegant spires of spruce and fir. It is a favorite watering hole for local wildlife, and it nourishes a vibrant growth of aquatic plants. A connecting path zigzags upward from the foot of the pond to reach the Upper Trail, bisecting the loop and offering shorter hike options for travelers who find themselves pressed for time.

The main trail follows the western shore of the pond and then ascends gradually through a series of pocket meadows. It soon reaches a quarrylike slope of broken rock. Unlike the sedimentary stone that forms the Cedar Breaks amphitheater, this stone is a much younger volcanic rock. Laid down as a thick bed of volcanic ash, it was transformed under great heat and pressure into a resistant stone known as welded tuff. Over the centuries water has worked its way into fissures in the tuff and then frozen and expanded, wedging boulders away from the parent rock. The resulting apron of rock debris is known as a talus slope. The loose boulders make an ideal nesting habitat for a variety of rodents. Look for badger-size yellow-bellied marmots, smaller pikas or "rock rabbits," and diminutive Uinta chipmunks.

The path soon climbs toward the Alpine Pond trailhead; turn south on the Upper Trail to complete the loop. The trail wends its way through a mature spruce-fir woodland. This forest is an important foraging area for the red squirrel, which harvests cones throughout the summer and hoards them in underground caches for use during the winter

CEDAR BREAKS
NATIONAL
MONUMENT

CEDAR BREAKS AMPHITHEATER

Rattle

Creek

Alpine Pond Trailhead

Alpine
Pond

148

Chessmen
Ridge

12

Chessmen

To Monument
Headquarters

months. Some caches are inevitably forgotten, and in favorable conditions the seeds within these lost cones can sprout and help renew the forest.

Numerous snags rise among the living trees in this area, the victims of frequent lightning storms that rage across the high Markagunt Plateau. To local wildlife these trees become even more valuable after they die: They support populations of insects that are a valuable food source and may also become homes for cavity-nesting mammals and birds. Two of the more prevalent cavity-nesting birds found in this area are the flicker and the mountain bluebird.

The trees give way to grassy glades, and sun-loving aspens thrive along the edges of the meadows. Conifers grow in clumps in this area, with skirts of their tiny offspring surrounding them on every side. Many of these "seedlings" are actually clones of the parent trees, thrown off when lower boughs took root in the soil and grew into independent trees.

After passing the cutoff trail that descends to Alpine Pond, the Upper Trail continues southward along the edge of the vast meadows that are so characteristic of the crest of the Markagunt Plateau. These meadows offer brilliant displays of wildflowers throughout the summer, highlighted by paintbrush and fleabane. Herds of deer sometimes graze here during autumn. The path ultimately finds its way back to the Chessmen Overlook, after an overall distance of 2.1 miles.

Key Points

- **0.0** Chessmen Overlook trailhead.
- **0.2** Trail splits. Follow Lower Trail, to the left.
- **0.6** Alpine Pond. Junction with cutoff to Upper Trail. Follow Lower Trail around the western shore of the pond.
- **1.1** Junction with short spur to Alpine Pond trailhead. Turn right onto Upper Trail to complete the loop.
- **1.5** Cutoff trail descends to Alpine Pond. Bear left.
- **2.1** Trail ends at Chessmen Overlook.

Bryce Canyon National Park

The towering hoodoos, spires, and natural bridges of Bryce Canyon National Park seem to deny all reason or explanation, leaving hikers gazing skyward with jaws agape in wondrous incredulity.

The forces that created Bryce Canyon are still at work today. The bedrock originated 60 million years ago, when southern Utah held a series of low-lying lakebeds. For millions of years, rivers deposited sediments into these lakebeds, eventually filling them and causing the lakes to dry out. The continual deposition of rocks, clays, and silts caused these materials to be compressed and form sedimentary rock layers. Some layers contained deposits of clays and silts, while other layers were rich in lime, dolomite, and carbonates. Throughout all of these layers are iron oxides and manganese compounds, lending hues of orange and purple to the stone. Over time these sediments hardened into rock known as the Claron Formation.

These geologic processes continued unchanged until about 16 million years ago, when powerful forces began to lift the Colorado Plateau. The stress caused by the uplift created countless joints or vertical cracks throughout the Claron Formation and caused southern Utah to fracture along several fault lines. Resulting from this uplifting force are the nine high plateaus of southern Utah.

Bryce Canyon is not so much a canyon as it is a series of amphitheaters created by erosional forces of the Paria River system along the edge of the Paunsaugunt Plateau. As the streams traveled eastward over the edge and down the slope of the plateau, the waters gained velocity and began to carry away bits of the Claron Formation. As this process continued, gullies cut deeply into the plateau, exposing layers of rock. These gully walls then became vulnerable to other forms of erosion, primarily through trickling water and the freeze-thaw cycle.

Visitors overlooking the canyon rim can see for themselves what time and geological forces have created, and adventurous and curious hikers can take advantage of the park's trails to experience Bryce Canyon on a more intimate level.

Day hikers will find numerous options to suit varying needs. Day hikes through the park range from 1-mile loops to 11-mile round-trip trails. One advantage of hiking in Bryce Canyon is that many of the trails intersect one another and can be connected to form loops. For instance, the Navajo Loop, Peekaboo Loop, and Queens Garden Trails can be combined with short excursions along connecting trails.

Before embarking on any hike in Bryce Canyon National Park, hikers should make sure they carry several essential items. First and foremost is water. Bryce Canyon is extremely hot and dry during summer. Water sources below the rim are severely limited and must be treated prior to consumption. As a rule, always carry ample water to last the duration of the hike, and then some. Carry sunscreen, eye protection, and a hat to prevent overexposure to the sun's rays. Since trails in Bryce Canyon traverse steep and rocky slopes, wear sturdy boots that provide ample support and protection. Always remember that Bryce Canyon sits at a high elevation; lowland visitors must allow themselves time to acclimate to the elevation. Finally, do not overestimate your abilities or overexert yourself while on the trails.

A shuttle runs between the shuttle area outside the park and trails in the main, upper amphitheater, which makes an excellent option to avoid crowded parking lots during busy summer weekends.

Most supplies and services can be found in the nearby town of Panguitch. However, Panguitch is a notorious speed trap: The police have been known to ticket out-of-state visitors traveling below the speed limit. If you don't have Utah license plates, we recommend steering clear.

13 Rim Trail

A popular trail above Bryce Canyon that connects all the scenic overlooks from Fairyland Point to Bryce Point.

Distance: 5.5 miles (8.9 km) one way
Hiking time: About 3 hours
Best season: Apr–Oct
Difficulty: Moderate
Water availability: Water is provided at various park restrooms.

Topo maps: Bryce Canyon, Bryce Point (Trails Illustrated)
Jurisdiction: Bryce Canyon National Park. See Appendix B for more information.

Finding the trailhead: From the Bryce Canyon Visitor Center, drive north 0.7 mile to the turnoff for Fairyland Point and park in the designated area. From the parking area walk east to the rim at Fairyland Point and follow the stone path south. The Rim Trail is also accessible from Sunrise, Sunset, Inspiration, and Bryce Points. GPS of start: N37° 38' 51.824" / W112° 8' 49.809"; GPS of finish: N37° 36' 9.335" / W112° 9' 15.860"

The Hike

This very popular path runs along the rim of Fairyland Canyon and Bryce Canyon. Many park visitors hike the Rim Trail since it is accessible from the park road at various lookout points and provides spectacular views of the spires and canyons below. Travelers can choose to hike the entire trail by starting from Fairyland Point or Bryce Point or break the hike up into smaller segments. Most of the pathway between Sunrise and Inspiration points is either paved or so well worn that portions are wheelchair accessible. However, steep gradients and uneven surfaces may make wheelchair access to some areas difficult.

From Fairyland Point follow the well-worn gravel path southward as it winds upward through a forest of juniper, ponderosa pine, Douglas fir, and bristlecone pine. For about a mile the path intermittently leaves the rim to pass along the westward slopes of hills, blocking views of Fairyland Canyon to the east. The trail emerges into a lightly forested area burned by the Park Service in fall 1995 as a controlled management burn. The path levels off along the rim and then turns southwest into the burn area.

Continuing westward, the trail descends across another slope, moving away from the rim. It eventually winds east to round the hill and emerges once again at the rim of the canyon. Northward views from this location encompass Boat Mesa and the Aquarius Plateau. Bristlecone Point, Canaan Mountain, the Kaiparowits Plateau, and Navajo Mountain can be seen to the east.

From here the path briefly levels out along the rim before ascending westward around another hill. Bristlecone pines grow from the barren, rocky slopes here. The trail eventually starts to descend, looping around to the northeast and again emerging at the canyon rim. From here the trail begins a gradual descent through a dense forest of conifers. The path levels off briefly and then begins to climb along the rim.

Next the path gradually descends toward a junction with the Fairyland Loop. At this junction turn left to begin the Fairyland Loop, or bear right to continue along the Rim Trail, which traverses an eastward-facing slope that overlooks the canyon. The trail then leaves the slope and descends to Sunrise Point, 0.25 mile south of the Fairyland junction.

Views of the Sinking Ship and Boat Mesa present themselves on the final approach to Sunrise Point. As the trail climbs a gradual slope to Sunrise Point, it meets the Queen's Garden Trail. Bear right to remain on the Rim Trail. Sunrise Point provides spectacular views of the Bryce Canyon amphitheater below.

Sunset Point is encountered about 0.5 mile south of Sunrise Point. Follow the path as it continues along the rim, providing excellent views of the south rim of Bryce Canyon. A juniper-pine forest with a ground cover of manzanita grows to the west of the trail. Wooden benches at various points along the path give visitors opportunities to relax and enjoy the wondrous scenery.

As the trail nears Sunset Point, northward views once again reveal Boat Mesa, the Sinking Ship, and the Aquarius Plateau. A junction with the Navajo Loop lies just north of Sunset Point. Thor's Hammer lies directly below the rim to the left (north) of the Navajo Loop.

From Sunset Point visitors can look down to see a small portion of the narrow rift called Wall Street. After taking in the view, follow the paved path southward. The numerous rifts and caverns of the Silent City await, directly below the rim to the south of Sunset Point. Across the canyon the Peekaboo Loop can be seen as it winds around the base of The Cathedral.

The Rim Trail soon meets a spur trail leading to Sunset Campground. Bear left and follow the Rim Trail as it leaves the rim and climbs a moderate grade. Below the trail to the west is a pine forest dominated by ponderosas but including limber pine as well. The trail levels off and quickly returns to the rim with the Silent City to the north and The Cathedral and Wall of Windows to the southeast.

The trail quickly winds around another small hill and returns to the rim once more before undertaking the steady climb to Inspiration Point and its three overlooks. As the trail approaches the first overlook, the Wall of Windows can be seen to the left (southeast). The northern horizon opens up dramatically as the trail continues to gain elevation. After a steady climb to the second Inspiration Point overlook, hikers can observe the bottom of Bryce Canyon and study the drainage pattern that flows eastward into Bryce Creek. The third Inspiration Point overlook is located on a spur trail at the top of the ascent. From this point one can see the Wall of Windows to the northwest and the town of Tropic in the opposite direction.

Returning along the spur back to the Rim Trail, through hikers should look for a trail sign that indicates the direction to Bryce Point. The trail now becomes a narrow, unpaved path. The path traverses a ridgeline, passing precariously steep cliffs and crossing a draw. Beyond the draw the narrow path winds up through a pleasant conifer stand. This stretch of trail overlooks the Wall of Windows and grotto formations in the canyon walls. The trail then leaves the rim and begins a gradual descent through a loose growth of conifers. It eventually approaches the rim just above the Wall of Windows and bends southward. Hikers can see more grottos and caverns in the rim wall below Bryce Point, to the southeast.

Once again the trail briefly leaves the rim and then returns to it and descends a series of switchbacks. At the bottom of the grade, the trail levels out and continues a gradual descent until it overlooks a draw. From here it makes a steady climb to Bryce Point. The final approach to Bryce Point is along a steep, westward-facing slope.

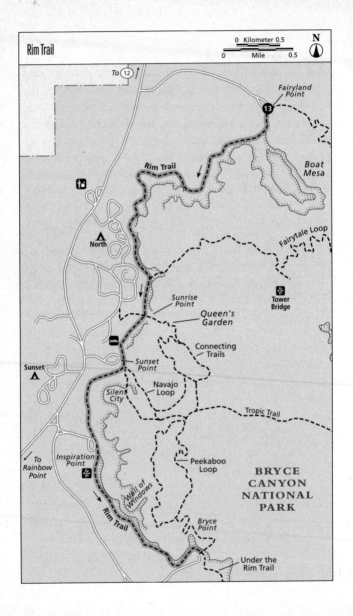

Before reaching its terminus at the two Bryce Point overlooks, the trail meets a spur trail to the Bryce Point parking lot. Turn left to reach the overlooks. These two vantage points provide excellent views northwest into Bryce Canyon, north toward the Aquarius Plateau, and northeast toward the Kaiparowits Plateau.

Key Points

0.0 Start at Fairyland Point.

2.2 Junction with Fairyland Loop. Bear right.

2.5 Sunrise Point.

3.0 Sunset Point.

3.8 Inspiration Point.

4.3 Wall of Windows Overlook.

5.5 Bryce Point.

14 **Queen's Garden Complex**

A short trail descending below the canyon rim.

Distance: 0.9 mile (1.4 km) one way

Hiking time: About 0.5 hour

Best season: Apr–Oct

Difficulty: Moderate

Water availability: None

Hazards: Steep slopes, loose gravel

Topo maps: Bryce Canyon, Bryce Point (Trails Illustrated)

Jurisdiction: Bryce Canyon National Park. See Appendix B for more information.

Finding the trailhead: From the Bryce Canyon Visitor Center, drive south 0.4 mile to the turnoff for Sunrise Point. Follow road signs to Sunrise Point and park in the designated area. From the parking area walk southeast along well-worn paths to the Queen's Garden trailhead. GPS: N37° 37' 41.462" / W112° 9' 51.146"

The Hike

The Queen's Garden Trail is a short, 0.9-mile route that drops about 320 feet below the canyon rim. Although the trail is not a loop, hikers can loop back up to the rim by combining a connecting trail with either branch of the Navajo Loop. Interesting rock formations along this popular path include Gulliver's Castle, the Queen's Castle, and Queen Elizabeth herself.

From the trailhead the trail descends along a slope below Sunrise Point. The path briefly traces a ridgeline but soon returns to a northward-facing slope. Early views include Boat Mesa, the Sinking Ship, and the Aquarius Plateau to the northeast; Bristlecone Point, Canaan Mountain, the

Queen's Garden Complex

To 12

North ▲

Fairyland Loop

Sunrise Point

14

Queen's Garden Trail

Queen's Garden Connector

Sunset ▲

Sunset Point

Navajo Loop

Tropic Trail

To Rainbow Point

Inspiration Point

Peekaboo Loop

Rim Trail

BRYCE CANYON NATIONAL PARK

Bryce Point

Kilometer
Mile

N

Kaiparowits Plateau, and Navajo Mountain show themselves in the east.

The trail continues along this slope until it bends to the south and descends a series of switchbacks. At the bottom of the grade, the path straightens out onto a ridgeline with Bryce Canyon below to the south and a conifer-filled draw to the north. The trail soon descends another set of switchbacks and levels off along a slope with the Aquarius Plateau and the Sinking Ship to the northeast. It then bends right and comes to a junction with the Tropic Trail; bear right to continue the Queen's Garden Trail.

The trail continues to descend via a series of short switchbacks to a tunnel cut through a wall of hoodoos. Beyond the tunnel ragged spires tower over the trail, which continues along the base of the formations, passes between two hoodoos, and again descends via switchbacks. The path straightens out above a draw and passes through another tunnel. Beyond the tunnel the trail bends south and traverses along the slopes overlooking another draw. The trail bends right, passes through a third tunnel, and joins the Navajo Loop Connecting Trail at the bottom of the canyon. Bear left to reach the Navajo Loop, or right to continue the Queen's Garden Trail.

The Queen Elizabeth formation and the end of the trail rise 50 feet west of the junction.

Key Points

0.0 Queen's Garden trailhead at Sunrise Point.

0.8 Junction with connecting trail to the Navajo Loop. Bear right.

0.9 Queen Elizabeth formation and end of trail.

15 Navajo Loop

A loop from Sunset Point down to the floor of Bryce Canyon and back again.

Distance: 1.4-mile (2.2 km) loop

Hiking time: About 1.5 hours

Best season: Apr–Oct

Difficulty: Moderate

Water availability: None

Topo maps: Bryce Point (Trails Illustrated)

Jurisdiction: Bryce Canyon National Park. See Appendix B for more information.

Finding the trailhead: The trail departs from a signpost at the central overlook point at Sunset Point. GPS: N37° 37' 17.082" / W112° 9' 55.660"

The Hike

This popular trail makes a short 1- to 2-hour loop from the rim at Sunset Point down to the floor of Bryce Canyon. The trail visits favorite hoodoo formations such as Wall Street, Twin Bridges, and Thor's Hammer.

From Sunset Point the trail immediately descends along a paved path with safety railings along the edges. After about 100 feet the railing ends and the path splits, with two trails heading off to the right (south) and one trail heading off to the left (east). The left-hand path is the eastern leg of the Navajo Loop; it will be discussed later in this description. The two right-hand paths consist of an upper and a lower trail.

The upper trail is a short spur to a window looking through a hoodoo wall down into the west portion of Bryce Canyon. The lower trail is the first leg of the Navajo Loop; it begins a rapid descent along a series of long and short switchbacks down to the canyon floor. At the bottom of the switchbacks, the trail straightens out and makes a gradual descent through Wall Street, where two towering Douglas firs have been growing in the depths of the rift for more than 750 years.

Upon emerging from Wall Street, hikers follow a wide pathway bordered by manzanita, juniper, and ponderosa pines. The end of the south leg of the Navajo Loop is identified by trail signs for the Peekaboo Loop Connecting Trail and the Queen's Garden Connecting Trail. Hikers can make a hard left turn to complete the remaining 0.6 mile of the Navajo Loop back up to Sunset Point, or connect with one of these other paths for a longer hike.

Continuing along the Navajo Loop (the left-hand path noted above), hikers gain enjoyable views of large hoodoo formations flanking both sides of the path. One such formation, Twin Bridges, is located on the right side of the trail at mile 1. Beyond Twin Bridges the path ascends a series of switchbacks to return to the rim. Look for Thor's Hammer to the north along this final section of trail.

Key Points

0.0   Navajo Loop trailhead at Sunset Point.

0.4   Wall Street.

0.6   Junction with Peekaboo Loop and Queen's Garden Connecting Trail. Turn left to complete the Navajo Loop.

1.0   Twin Bridges formation on north side of trail.

1.4   Trail arrives back at Sunset Point.

16 Peekaboo Loop

A loop for hikers and horses through the pink limestone formations below the rim of Bryce Canyon.

Distance: 5.5-mile (8.9 km) loop	**Topo maps:** Bryce Point (Trails Illustrated)
Hiking time: About 3 hours	**Jurisdiction:** Bryce Canyon National Park. See Appendix B for more information.
Best season: Apr–Oct	
Difficulty: Moderate	
Water availability: None	

Finding the trailhead: From the Bryce Canyon Visitor Center, drive south 1.6 miles to a turnoff for Inspiration and Bryce Points. Follow road signs to Bryce Point and park in the designated area. The Bryce Point trailhead is at the north corner of the parking lot. GPS: N37° 36' 9.335" / W112° 9' 15.860"

The Hike

A short connector begins at Bryce Point and descends below the rim to connect with the Peekaboo Loop, a hiker and horse trail that winds around hoodoo formations below Inspiration Point and Bryce Point. Views along this trail include the popular Wall of Windows, The Three Wisemen, The Organ, and The Cathedral as well as eastward views beyond the canyon toward the Aquarius Plateau, Canaan Mountain, and the Kaiparowits Plateau.

The trail departs from the north corner of the Bryce Point parking lot. From the sidewalk follow the trail as it descends southeast along a slope below the parking lot. The trail soon meets a junction with the Under the Rim Trail; bear right to follow this trail toward the Hat Shop formations.

To reach the Peekaboo Loop, turn left and follow the trail as it descends northeast along a gravel path. Bristlecone and limber pines grow along the trail as it heads down a series of short switchbacks. At the bottom of the grade, the trail straightens out along a slope beneath towering white cliffs of limestone. Northward views here include Bryce Canyon, below, and Boat Mesa rising in the distance.

The trail drops until it reaches a man-made tunnel. Beyond the tunnel the pathway levels off and continues northwest beneath Bryce Point overlook and several grotto formations. Rockfalls commonly make the path extremely narrow and rocky, making for unstable footing.

Continuing northwest, the trail passes a large hoodoo wall and begins another gradual descent. The Wall of Windows lies to the west of the trail as it turns a switchback and then bends to the right. Hoodoos directly below this portion of the trail provide good examples of resistant, lime-rich layers capping the formation and protecting the weaker layers below from erosion. The trail winds down the slope and traverses beneath these caprock formations.

Just beyond the hoodoos the trail comes to a junction with the Peekaboo Loop. Turn left (west) at the junction to quickly reach the Peekaboo Loop horse corrals and pit toilets. Then turn right and follow the trail as it heads down a switchbacked slope, passing bristlecone and limber pines along the way. The trail straightens and continues to drop gradually along the west side of a draw. Pink hoodoos line the draw's sides as ponderosa pine, juniper, and manzanita grow in the bottom.

The path eventually traverses northwest across the draw and begins a slow ascent across a series of washes and then follows switchbacks up to a tunnel cut into the ridgetop.

Beyond the tunnel the trail bends left and continues up the opposite (north) slope of the ridge. Hoodoos decorate the ridgetops as the trail levels off and winds along the slopes. Other views include Bryce Point and grotto formations to the south of the trail.

The trail eventually makes a short ascent and cuts between two hoodoo formations. At the top of the climb, the rifts and caverns of the Silent City can be seen ahead to the north. The trail begins to descend at the base of The Cathedral. It then straightens out and follows the upper left side of a draw, with Boat Mesa rising on the northern horizon.

Another set of switchbacks drops hikers down into the draw. From here the trail goes down the draw to a junction with the Navajo Loop Connecting Trail. Bear right to reach the Navajo Loop; turn left to return to the Bryce Point trail via the Peekaboo Loop.

The main route heads up a gradual slope here, providing overlooking views of a wash bed and the Navajo Loop to the right (west). The path ascends steadily along slopes until it passes through a small cavern. Afterward it levels off somewhat and begins to wind around pink limestone formations above the canyon floor.

After several small ascents and descents, the path passes through a man-made arch and into a small grotto with large hoodoo walls towering above. The trail descends through this cavern via a series of short switchbacks. At the bottom of the switchbacks, it emerges from the cavern with a close-up view of the Wall of Windows to the right. The trail briefly traverses the base of the Wall of Windows. Looking up at the canyon rim from here, hikers can see grottos in the cliffs.

Beyond the Wall of Windows, the trail descends to the canyon floor, where a horse corral and pit toilets are located

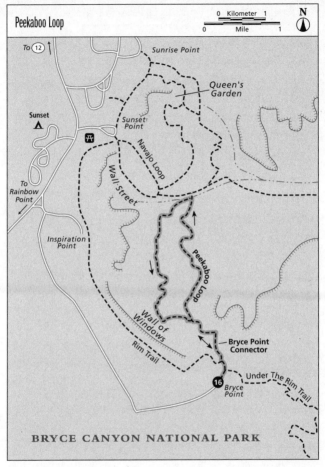

To (12)

Peekaboo Loop

0 Kilometer 1
0 Mile 1

N

Sunrise Point

Queen's Garden

Sunset ▲

Sunset Point

Navajo Loop

Wall Street

To Rainbow Point

Inspiration Point

Peekaboo Loop

Wall of Windows

Rim Trail

Bryce Point Connector

16 Bryce Point

Under The Rim Trail

BRYCE CANYON NATIONAL PARK

(this is the only trail in Bryce Canyon where pit toilets are provided along the route). The junction with the Bryce Point Trail, which will take you back to your starting point, is located slightly uphill from the horse corral.

Key Points

0.0   Trailhead at Bryce Point.

0.1   Junction with the Under the Rim Trail. Turn left.

1.0   Junction with the Peekaboo Loop. Turn right.

2.2   Junction with the Navajo Loop Connecting Trail. Turn left.

2.5   The Cathedral.

3.1   The Wall of Windows.

3.6   Horse corral.

4.5   Return to Bryce Point Trail. Turn right.

5.4   Junction with the Under the Rim Trail. Turn right.

5.5   Bryce Point.

17 Bristlecone Loop

A short loop trail above the rim at Rainbow Point.

Distance: 1 mile (1.6 km) loop	**Topo maps:** Rainbow Point (Trails
Hiking time: About 0.5 hour	Illustrated)
Best season: Apr–Oct	**Jurisdiction:** Bryce Canyon
Difficulty: Easy	National Park. See Appendix B
Water availability: None	for more information.

Finding the trailhead: From the Bryce Canyon Visitor Center, drive 16.8 miles south to Rainbow Point. Follow the sidewalk to the southeast side of the parking lot to the Bristlecone Loop trailhead sign. An additional trailhead sign is located to the left of the restrooms. GPS: N37° 28' 25.393" / W112° 14' 30.337"

The Hike

This short loop stays entirely above the canyon rim as it traverses a subalpine fir forest. The trail is named after the bristlecone pine, which is found more frequently along this trail than along other trails in Bryce Canyon National Park. Bristlecone pine can be identified by the foxtail tufts of needles growing at the tips of its limbs. It can survive on high, windy ridges and can weather prolonged periods of drought. Due to its tenacity the bristlecone pine has a tremendous lifespan. A California specimen has been dated at more than 4,500 years old.

From the trailhead the path winds southeast through dense stands of white fir, Douglas fir, and ponderosa pine. The path loops out to the cliffs and the canyon rim. Bristlecone pines grow atop the open, windy cliffs along the rim.

Bristlecone Loop

N

To Park Headquarters

Under the Rim Trail

Rainbow Point

17

Park Road

The Promontory

Corral Hollow

Riggs Spring Loop

Yovimpa Pass

BRYCE CANYON NATIONAL PARK

Kilometer 0.5
0
Mile 0.5
0

As the trail returns to Rainbow Point, it intersects the Under the Rim Trail. Trail signs along the route direct hikers back to the starting point.

Key Points

0.0   Rainbow Point trailhead. Follow the path south.

0.1   Junction with Riggs Spring Loop.

0.8   Junction with the Under the Rim Trail. Follow trail signs for Rainbow Point to return to the trailhead.

1.0   Trail returns to Rainbow Point trailhead.

18 Mossy Cave

A short hike at the northeastern end of Bryce Canyon National Park.

Distance: 0.4 mile one way
Hiking time: About 0.25 hour
Best season: Apr–Oct
Difficulty: Easy
Water availability: Water Canyon typically holds water.

Hazards: Slippery stream crossings
Topo maps: Tropic Canyon (Trails Illustrated)
Jurisdiction: Bryce Canyon National Park. See Appendix B for more information.

Finding the trailhead: Drive UT 12 east from the junction with UT 63 to a marked pulloff on the south side of the road, 1.2 miles west of the park's east entrance. GPS: N37° 39' 50.068" / W112° 6' 33.972"

The Hike

This trail offers a short stroll into the reddish pinnacles of Bryce Canyon from UT 12, offering a smaller-scale sampler of the grandeur to the south for travelers who do not wish to make the side trip into the main part of the park. The stream flows found here are not natural; pioneering settlers diverted water from the Sevier River into Water Canyon via a series of canals to feed croplands around Tropic.

The trail begins by following Water Canyon up into the breaks, with a wall of impressive pinnacles rising to the west. Soon the path reaches the first of two stream crossings. The crossings are usually easy rock-hops, but they can be tricky during spring runoff. Near the upper crossing look up to

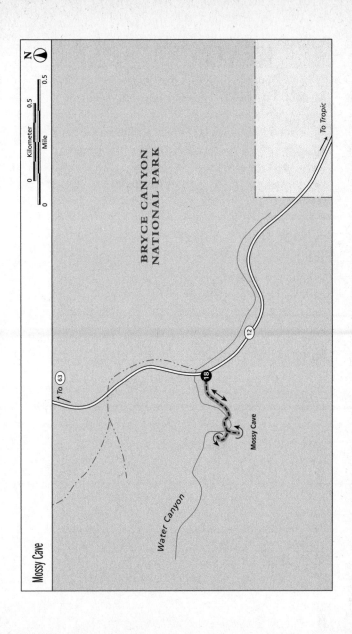

Mossy Cave

BRYCE CANYON
NATIONAL PARK

Water Canyon

Mossy Cave

To 63

12

To Tropic

N

0   Kilometer   0.5
0   Mile   0.5

view the natural arches and window walls in the cliffs to the west. Once the second crossing is made, a short climb leads to a T-intersection. To the right a short stroll leads to a 10-foot waterfall. To the left a brief but steep climb leads to Mossy Cave itself. This spacious alcove has been chiseled out by groundwater seeping through weaknesses in the bedrock. In winter the seeps feed impressive icicle gardens, while in summer the water provides sustenance for a vivid growth of mosses.

Hidden Treasures of the Paunsaugunt Country

Bryce Canyon National Park occupies only a tiny corner of the vast Paunsaugunt Plateau, rimmed with rugged country that falls largely within the public domain. Countless hidden nooks and crannies here offer outstanding scenery, whether the view features the eroded red hoodoos of the uplands or the spectacular white cliffs of the Navajo Formation that gird the plateau's lower reaches. Most of these areas receive very low levels of visitation. It is here that travelers are most likely to avoid crowds and experience the wild solitude of a primeval landscape.

Most of the land falls under the direction of the Bureau of Land Management, which has local headquarters in Kanab. Several short day-hiking routes explore the western face of the Elkheart Cliffs.

19 Red Canyon Loop

A day-hiking route through Red Canyon encompassing portions of the Cassidy, Rich, and Ledge Point Trails in Dixie National Forest.

Distance: 4-mile (6.4 km) loop
Hiking time: About 2 hours
Best season: Apr–Oct
Difficulty: Moderate
Water availability: None
Hazards: Steep slopes, rocky surfaces

Topo maps: Wilson Peak, Casto Canyon
Jurisdiction: Powell Ranger District, Dixie National Forest. See Appendix B for more information.

Finding the trailhead: From US 89 drive east on UT 12. Continue 1 mile east from the Red Canyon Visitor Center to a paved turnoff for the Cassidy trailhead on the north side of UT 12. A parking area, horse corral, information board, and pit toilet are located at the trailhead. GPS: N37° 44' 41.357" / W112° 18' 3.540"

The Hike

This moderate route is pieced together with portions of the Cassidy, Rich, and Ledge Point Trails, making a loop through Red Canyon. These trails are also used by horse parties from April through October. Hikers who encounter horses on the trail should step aside and yield the right-of-way.

The route begins at the Cassidy trailhead at the northwest end of the parking lot. The path heads north, paralleling a wash through an arid landscape of ponderosa pine, limber pine, manzanita, and juniper. The terrain is rugged; pink limestone scree slopes border the wash. Like those of

Bryce Canyon and the Cedar Breaks, the formations visible through Red Canyon are predominantly white and pink limestone from the Claron Formation. About 0.5 mile up the wash, the first pink limestone hoodoo formations come into view.

About 0.8 mile from the trailhead, hikers reach a first junction with the Rich Trail. Bear right, staying on the Cassidy Trail. The trail continues along the stream course to a confluence of several washes. Here the trail turns left and heads up a gradual-to-moderate slope to surmount a small hill. The path briefly follows the ridgeline. As you make upward progress, notice the resistant rock formations along the ridges to the left and right. Douglas firs grow in these higher elevations.

While still up in the high country, the Cassidy Trail reaches a second intersection with the Rich Trail. Break from the Cassidy Trail and follow the Rich Trail to the left (south). This portion of trail goes through a saddle and then descends along a draw that lies just west of the ridge that bears the Cassidy Trail. Along the descent the trail passes by The Gap, a wash between two resistant buttes.

Beyond The Gap the trail ascends partway up another wash and then cuts across to another saddle, heading toward the Ledge Point Trail. The Ledge Point Trail is a horseshoe loop that intersects with the Rich Trail at two points. The loop brings hikers to Ledge Point, a picturesque overlook of the Red Canyon area with UT 12 visible below and to the south.

Follow the right (east) leg of the horseshoe loop back to the Rich Trail. Turn right and descend a slope that passes under cliffs of variegated sandstone above a watercourse. This portion of the trail is quite rocky, with gravel and

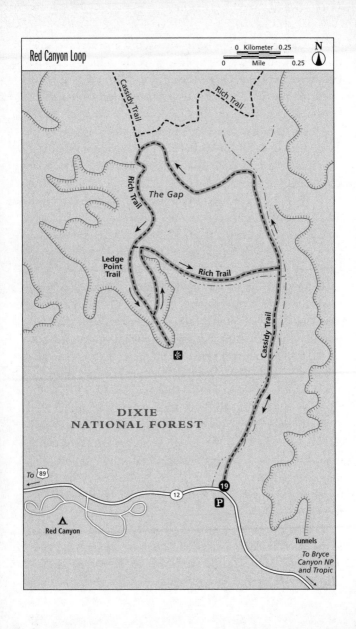

Red Canyon Loop

0 Kilometer 0.25
0 Mile 0.25

N

Cassidy Trail

Rich Trail

Rich Trail

The Gap

Ledge Point Trail

Rich Trail

Cassidy Trail

DIXIE NATIONAL FOREST

To 89

12

19

P

Red Canyon

Tunnels

To Bryce Canyon NP and Tropic

cobblestones. The trail briefly parallels the wash below and then descends rapidly to the streambed via a series of steep switchbacks. Along this portion of the trail are good examples of pink hoodoos and alcoves that border the wash. At the end of the draw, the path rejoins the Cassidy Trail. Backtrack southward along this portion of trail to return to the trailhead.

Key Points

0.0   Start at the trailhead.

0.8   Junction with the Rich Trail. Stay right on the Cassidy Trail.

1.7   Second junction with the Rich Trail. Turn left onto it.

2.1   Junction with the Ledge Point Trail. Turn right for a spur loop.

3.2   Junction with the Cassidy Trail. Turn right.

4.0   Arrive back at the trailhead.

20 Red Hollow

An out-and-back wilderness route up a short, picturesque canyon.

Distance: 2 miles (3.2 km)
out-and-back
Hiking time: About 1 hour
Best season: Apr–Oct
Difficulty: Easy
Water availability: None

Hazards: Some scrambling over
uneven surfaces, flash flood
danger
Topo maps: Orderville, Glendale
Jurisdiction: Bureau of Land
Management, Kanab Field
Office. See Appendix B for more
information.

Finding the trailhead: From Mt. Carmel Junction, follow US 89 north to Orderville. Turn right on 100 East Street at the Centennial School. Turn left on Red Hollow Drive. Drive 0.15 mile to a sand/gravel road. Follow the sand road 0.3 mile to a small turnout where a cement reservoir atop a small foothill should be in view. The hike begins by heading into the opening of a small canyon that is overlooked by pad-mounted transformers and a cement reservoir. GPS: N37° 16' 14.552" / W112° 37' 49.200"

The Hike

As the route enters the mouth of the canyon, a high bank presents itself on the left side. It soon gives way to red cliffs that extend down to the canyon floor. The canyon soon splits into two short branches, each of which invites further exploration. Both branches are wooded with Gambel oak, juniper, and ponderosa pine. Hikers should not attempt to climb onto the sloping canyon walls; they may be easy to ascend, but they are almost impossible to get back down.

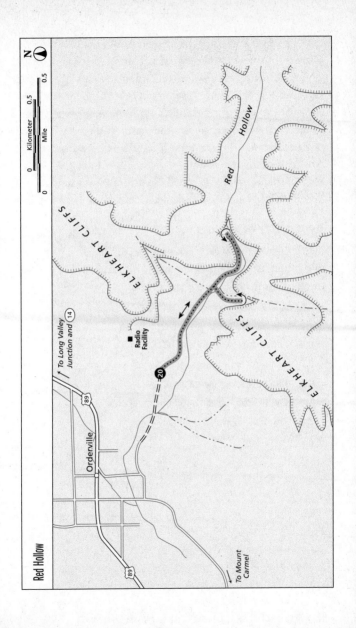

Red Hollow

The south branch of the canyon breaks away to the right and has a somewhat narrow watercourse. Sheer cliffs of red sandstone form the walls of this side canyon. Cobblestones and sand line the narrow watercourse, making for easy traveling. At the end of this branch are some interesting natural arch formations overhanging the wash. At the very headwall of the canyon, a freestanding leaf of stone has been carved out of the cliffs by erosion.

The main branch is called Red Hollow. Heading up it, hikers will find crimson walls that slant into the canyon floor on the left, while overhanging walls with solution holes rise on the right. The walls of this branch narrow abruptly to a width of 6 feet or so and become impassable after a distance of 0.8 mile from the parking area. This is the end of the trek; travelers must now retrace their route.

Key Points

0.0 End of improved road.

0.7 Confluence with wash coming in from the right (south).

0.9 Headwall of southern canyon.

1.0 End of main canyon and turnaround point.

2.0 Arrive back at road.

21 Sugar Knoll with Red Cave Option

A day hike to Sugar Knoll with an option to Red Cave.

Distance: 2.1 miles (3.4 km) to
Sugar Knoll; 1.8 miles (2.9 km)
to Red Cave, one way
Hiking time: About 1.5 hours
one way to either destination
Best season: Mar-Nov
Difficulty: Moderate
Water availability: The potholes
within Red Cave always contain
murky water.

Hazards: Extreme flash flood
danger within Red Cave
Topo map: Mount Carmel
Jurisdiction: Bureau of Land
Management, Kanab Field
Office. See Appendix B for more
information.

Finding the trailhead: From Orderville drive south on US 89 to
the historic schoolhouse at mile 83.5. Park here and hike north along
the highway for 0.2 mile to a dirt road that runs eastward to the river.
This road is the beginning of the hike. GPS: N37° 14' 50.227" /
W112° 39' 43.057"

The Hike

This route offers several manageable day-hiking options, visiting the spectacular high country at the base of the Elkheart
Cliffs. These destinations are well known to local residents
but receive little attention from others, so these hikes offer a
fairly good opportunity for solitude. The Sugar Knoll route
travels right to the base of the Elkheart Cliffs, while the Red
Cave route visits an impossibly narrow slot canyon carved
into red sandstone.

The hike initially follows a dirt road that runs eastward
across the Long Valley. It soon makes an ankle-deep ford of

the East Fork of the Virgin River. On the far bank the road swings north along the river for a time and then jogs east again to reach a corral and gravel pit at the base of the hills. The route then follows a jeep track that rounds the corral on a northward heading and soon climbs to the top of a low plateau. Along the way are fine views of the Long Valley's fertile bottomlands.

Once the jeep road reaches the top of the plateau, a scrub forest of juniper allows only brief glimpses of the bone-white Elkheart Cliffs to the east. These cliffs, which are of the same Navajo sandstone as Zion Canyon, guard the edge of the Paunsaugunt Plateau. The jeep trail meanders through the scrub and breaks out onto a sagebrush flat just before reaching the Bureau of Land Management land boundary.

The track then makes its way to the edge of a steep bluff. Far below, a sandy wash issues from the red rock layers that underlie the Elkheart Cliffs. This arroyo is known as Sand Wash, and at its head is the slot canyon known locally as Red Cave. A second jeep trail soon drops away to the right to begin a journey up this canyon (see Red Cave Option, below).

Bear left at the fork for Sugar Knoll as the main jeep trail continues to climb gently toward the base of the cliffs. After 1.4 miles the jeep road ends and a rough trail bears east-northeast toward a red rock hoodoo. Follow this trail as it climbs across the slickrock to reach an overlook that offers a sweeping view of Sugar Knoll, with the Elkheart Cliffs providing a stunning backdrop. The junipers fall away as the trail drops onto sand dunes that have been stabilized by a growth of sagebrush, manzanita, and Gambel oak.

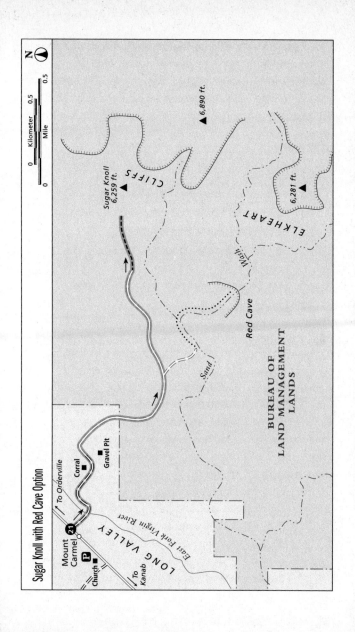

Sugar Knoll with Red Cave Option

Expect sandy hiking conditions as the trail covers the remaining distance to the base of Sugar Knoll. Here, beneath a small blowout cave in the bedrock, the path splits into a tangle of sandy avenues that entice further exploration along the base of this striking butte of wind-sculpted sandstone.

Key Points

0.0   Dirt road departs US 89.

0.2   Road fords the East Fork of the Virgin River.

0.4   Gravel pit. Follow jeep trail to the north.

1.1   Jeep trail enters BLM lands.

1.2   Jeep trail splits; bear left. (*Option:* Turn right for the 0.6-mile trail to Red Cave.)

1.8   Jeep trail ends. Follow rough path to the northeast.

2.1   Base of Sugar Knoll.

Red Cave Option

This moderate trail adds about 1.2 miles round-trip to your hike. From the bluff-top junction of jeep trails, follow the track to the right (southeast) that descends steeply into the valley of Sand Wash. As its name implies, the wash is a wide avenue of sand that has been deposited by eons of flash flooding. Traveling is easy as the route follows the wash upward toward its source, an impossibly narrow declivity in the red lower layers of Navajo sandstone. This is the slot canyon called Red Cave, and hikers can penetrate it for only a short distance without vigorous climbing.

Deep pools of water form in the floor of the cleft and are always cold—wear a wetsuit for extended exploration. Whorled walls rise up to block the sky, and the canyon floor is only wide enough to admit travelers in single file. This narrow chasm is a death trap when waters reach flood stage, since hikers have no way to climb upward. Visitors should carefully monitor the weather conditions and enter the slot canyon only if cloudless skies are a certainty.

When you return to the main trail, take a right for Sugar Knoll or turn left to return to the trailhead.

22 Dianas Throne

An out-and-back day hike along jeep trails

Distance: 2.1 miles (3.4 km) out-and-back
Hiking time: About 1 hour
Best season: March–May
Elevation gain: 342 feet
Difficulty: Easy
Water availability: None

Hazards: Extremely hot and dry
Topo map: USGS Mount Carmel
Jurisdiction: Bureau of Land Management, Kanab Field Office. See Appendix B for more information.

Finding the trailhead: Take US 89 west from Kanab or east from Mount Carmel to mile 76.4, just west of the highway's summit. Drive north on a gravel road to a junction with the old highway bed, now a gravel road. Park here; the hike begins on the gated jeep trail (marked 106P) that runs north from this junction. GPS: N37° 10' 51.71" / W112° 38' 4.78"

The Hike

Dianas Throne is a majestic tower of white Navajo sandstone that rises at the southern tip of the Elkheart Cliffs. This often sandy hike follows jeep trails that remain open to vehicle travel, so you may encounter motorized users along the route.

The hike begins with a sandy uphill through piñons and junipers, bearing for the western face of Dianas Throne. After a short climb you will meet a power line; turn left onto jeep trail 106L. Follow this route up a gentle grade to a saddle, then turn right onto 106Q, which you will follow for the remainder of the hike. The trees thin out now for

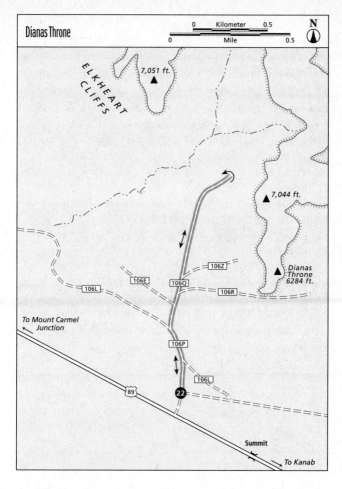

unobstructed views of Dianas Throne, as well as the stone temples of Zion National Park on the western skyline. The understory here is a mixture of old sagebrush, rabbitbrush, and Mormon tea grown large in the absence of fire. The sandy jeep trail rises gently beside the west face of Dianas Throne and then curves into the alcove behind it. Upon striking a wash, it climbs briskly eastward to reach the end of motorized travel. From here, you can hike north up a ridgelet of pink sand to view the yellow- and rose-colored sandstone at the base of the Elkheart Cliffs. Note the contrasting diagonal bedding of the sandstone, known as "crossbedding," indicating that the sand was deposited in the form of windblown dunes before it solidified into rock.

Key Points

0.0	Begin hike. Hike north along jeep trail 106P.
0.1	Route reaches power line at junction with jeep trail 106L. Turn left.
0.3	Junction. Turn right onto jeep trail 106Q.
0.4	Junction with jeep trail 106E. Continue straight ahead.
0.5	Junction with jeep trail 106R. Continue straight ahead.
0.6	Junction with jeep trail 106Z. Continue straight ahead.
1.0	Jeep trail ends. Hike north to top of ridge. Turn around.
2.1	Return to start.

23 Coral Pink Sand Dunes

A day-hiking loop onto the ridges overlooking the dynamic Coral Pink Sand Dunes, returning through the dune fields themselves.

Distance: 2.5-mile (4 km) loop
Hiking time: About 2 hours
Best season: Apr–Nov
Difficulty: Moderately strenuous
Water availability: None
Hazards: Steep slopes with uneven footing

Topo map: Yellow Jacket Canyon
Jurisdiction: Bureau of Land Management, Kanab Field Office; Coral Pink Sand Dunes State Park. See Appendix B for more information.

Finding the trailhead: From Mount Carmel Junction drive south on US 89 to a sign marked coral pink sand dunes. Turn right on CR 1850 and drive 9.3 miles to a large, open area used for four-wheel-drive recreation on the left (east) side of the road. GPS: N37° 3' 55.850" / W112° 42' 16.781"

The Hike

More than half of the Coral Pink Sand Dunes are administered by the State of Utah as a state park. A state park campground and fee area are located in the southern section of the dunes. The dunes are used frequently by off-road vehicles. Hikers are also welcome but should exercise caution with this in mind.

The Coral Pink Sand Dunes offer an infinite array of possible route choices. The dunes occupy a long, narrow valley overlooked by sandstone hills to the east. As a result of prevailing winds, the dunes are oriented along an east-west axis. Travel is easiest along the axis of the dunes; hikers on a north–south heading will face numerous up and downs. A few loosely defined jeep tracks trace the edges of the dunes, but the heart of this miniature Sahara is essentially trailless. Our route climbs onto the ridges west of the dunes for an aerial view before descending into the heart of the dunes for the return trip.

From the parking area head southeast over the sand dunes toward the sandstone hills bordering the valley. These hills are wooded in an open scrub of ponderosa pine and juniper. Wherever possible stay on the four-wheel-drive tracks as you walk for easiest traveling. This will spare the delicate vegetation growing on the unstable slopes of the dunes. Watch the undisturbed surface of the sand for animal tracks and patterns made by the wind.

As you gain elevation and approach the sandstone foothills, notice that the dunes are partially stabilized by populations of ponderosa pine, sagebrush, yucca, and a variety of small desert plants. As the route climbs into the hills, limber pine, Gambel oak, and manzanita populations become prevalent.

Once up on the sandstone, head south along the foothills toward a gorge that penetrates the rock. This portion of the trek provides an excellent vantage point from which to look out over the dunes and study their patterns. Just before the gorge a few shallow washes head southward. Explore these, but proceed with caution—the washes end abruptly with a rapid descent into the gorge.

Descend into the dunes, choosing a route slightly north of the gorge. Investigate your route before beginning a descent in order to avoid thickets of Gambel oak and manzanita. Spending a few minutes studying the east-west

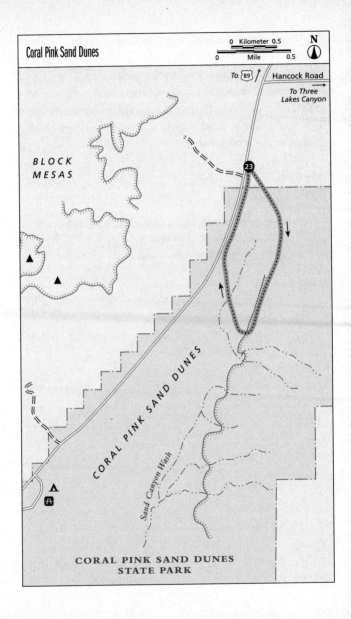

Coral Pink Sand Dunes

0 Kilometer 0.5
0 Mile 0.5

N

To ⁑89⁑
Hancock Road
To Three
Lakes Canyon

**BLOCK
MESAS**

23

CORAL PINK SAND DUNES

Sand Canyon Wash

**CORAL PINK SAND DUNES
STATE PARK**

pattern of the dunes will help you end your descent within a trough or on the crest of a dune. The trough or crest can then be followed back toward the parking area.

Sagebrush flats and a barbed-wire fence guard the western border of the state park. Angle northwest to encounter this fence and follow it north through the sagebrush to return to the parking area.

Key Points

0.0   Start at the parking area.

1.3   Deep gorge through the sandstone hills. Turn west and descend into the sand dunes.

2.5   Route returns to the parking area.

Note for Paunsagunt Country

Hiking with Your Dog

While dogs are not allowed on the trails in Zion and Bryce Canyon National Parks or in Cedar Breaks National Monument, they are welcome on Bureau of Land Management trails—Paunsagunt Country, hikes 19 through 23 in this book. As you know, our canine pals make great trail buddies because they never complain and always make good company.

Before you plan outdoor adventures with your dog, make sure he's in shape for the trail. Take him on your daily runs or walks. Also, be sure he has a firm grasp of the basics of canine etiquette and behavior, and that he can sit, lie down, stay, and come on command. Purchase collapsible water and dog food bowls for your dog. If you are hiking on rocky terrain or in the snow, you can purchase footwear for your dog that will protect his feet from cuts and bruises.

Once on the trail, keep your dog under control. You can buy a flexi-lead that allows your dog to go exploring along the trail, while allowing you the ability to reel him in should another hiker approach or should he decide to chase a rabbit. Always obey leash laws and be sure to bury your dog's waste or pack it in resealable plastic bags.

Appendix A: Hiking Tips

Hiking with Children

Hiking with children is all about seeing and experiencing nature through their eyes. Kids like to explore and have fun. They like to stop and point out bugs and plants, look under rocks, jump in puddles, and throw sticks. If you're taking a toddler or young child on a hike, start with a trail that you're familiar with. Trails that have interesting things for kids, like piles of leaves to play in or a small stream to wade through during the summer, will make the hike much more enjoyable for them and will keep them from getting bored.

You can keep your child's attention if you have a strategy before starting on the trail. Using games is not only an effective way to keep a child's attention, it's also a great way to teach him or her about nature. Quiz children on the names of plants and animals. If your children are old enough, let them carry their own daypacks filled with treats and a favorite (small) toy. So that you are sure to go at their pace and not yours, let them lead the way. Playing follow the leader works particularly well when you have a group of children. Have each child take a turn at being the leader.

Getting into Shape

Unless you want to be sore—and possibly have to shorten your trip or vacation—be sure to get in shape before a big hike. If you're terribly out of shape, start a walking program early, preferably eight weeks in advance. Start with a fifteen-minute walk during your lunch hour or after work and gradually increase your walking time to an hour. You should also increase your elevation gain. Walking briskly up hills really strengthens your leg muscles and gets your heart rate up. If you work in a storied office building, take the stairs instead of the elevator. If you prefer going to a gym, walk the treadmill or use a stair machine. You can further increase your strength and endurance by walking with a loaded backpack. Stationary exercises you might consider are squats, leg lifts, sit-ups, and push-ups. Other good ways to get in shape include biking, running, aerobics, and, of course, short hikes. Stretching before and after a hike keeps muscles flexible and helps avoid injuries.

Appendix B: Managing Agencies

Bureau of Land Management
Kanab Field Office
669 S. Hwy. 89A
Kanab, UT 84741
(435) 644-1200
www.blm.gov/ut/st/en/fo/kanab.html

St. George Field Office
345 E. Riverside Dr.
St. George, UT 84790
(435) 688-3200
www.blm.gov/ut/st/en/fo/st__george.html

Forest Service
Powell Ranger District
225 E. Center
Panguitch, UT 84759
(435) 676-9300

Supervisor
Dixie National Forest
1789 North Wedgewood Lane
Cedar City, UT 84721
(435) 865-3700
www.fs.usda.gov/dixie

National Park Service
Bryce Canyon National Park
PO Box 640201
Bryce Canyon, UT 84764-0201
(435) 834–5322
www.nps.gov/brca

Cedar Breaks National Monument
2390 W. Hwy. 56, Suite 11
Cedar City, UT 84720
(435) 586-9451
www.nps.gov/cebr

Zion National Park
Springdale, UT 84767-1099
(435) 772-3256
www.nps.gov/zion

State of Utah
Coral Pink Sand Dunes State Park
PO Box 95
Kanab, UT 84741-0095
(435) 648-2800
www.utah.com/stateparks/coral_pink.htm

Appendix C: Hiker Checklist

Most hikers realize the importance of a good checklist once they are on the trail: What you have forgotten to pack may turn out to be only an inconvenience, or it may pose a serious problem. A good checklist will help you remember the essentials.

The list below is only a suggested list. Use it to create your own, based on the nature of your hike and personal needs. Items will vary depending on whether you are day hiking or backpacking into remote country. If you are carrying supplies on your back, select items judiciously, with weight in mind.

Clothing

- ❑ dependable rain parka
- ❑ wind-resistant jacket
- ❑ wetsuit (for canyon wading in cold weather)
- ❑ thermal underwear
- ❑ shorts
- ❑ long pants
- ❑ cap or hat
- ❑ wool shirt or sweater
- ❑ warm jacket
- ❑ extra socks
- ❑ underwear
- ❑ lightweight shirts
- ❑ T-shirts
- ❑ wool gloves

Footwear

- ❏ comfortable hiking boots
- ❏ lightweight camp shoes
- ❏ water shoes or sandals

Bedding

- ❏ sleeping bag
- ❏ foam pad or air mattress
- ❏ pillow (deflating)
- ❏ ground cloth (plastic or nylon)
- ❏ dependable tent

Cooking

- ❏ 1-quart plastic water containers
- ❏ 1-gallon collapsible water container
- ❏ backpack stove with extra fuel
- ❏ funnel or pour spout for fuel
- ❏ aluminum foil
- ❏ cooking pot
- ❏ bowl or plate
- ❏ spoon, fork, knife, spatula
- ❏ butane lighter or matches in a waterproof container

Food & Drink

- ❑ cereal
- ❑ bread and/or crackers
- ❑ trail mix
- ❑ margarine
- ❑ powdered soups
- ❑ salt, pepper, spices
- ❑ main-course meals
- ❑ snacks
- ❑ coffee, tea, hot chocolate
- ❑ powdered milk
- ❑ drink mixes

Photography

- ❑ camera
- ❑ film
- ❑ accessories
- ❑ dry bag

Miscellaneous

- ❑ maps, compasses
- ❑ wading staff
- ❑ toilet paper and PVC "poop tube"
- ❑ small trowel or shovel
- ❑ toothbrush and toothpaste
- ❑ water filter or purifier
- ❑ first-aid kit

- survival kit
- pocket knife
- insect repellent
- flashlight, with spare batteries and bulb
- candles
- extra plastic bags to pack out trash
- biodegradable soap
- towel/washcloth
- waterproof covering for pack
- binoculars
- watch
- sewing kit
- this hiking guide

About the Authors

Erik Molvar discovered backpacking while working on a volunteer trail crew in the North Cascades of Washington. His experiences led him to choose a career in the outdoors, and he soon found himself studying wildlife biology at the University of Montana. His studies there were followed by a master of science degree from the University of Alaska, Fairbanks, where his groundbreaking research on the behavior and ecology of moose was published in several international journals. Erik is currently the director of Biodiversity Conservation Alliance, a nonprofit conservation group in Wyoming. His other FalconGuides include *Hiking Arizona's Cactus Country*, *Hiking the Bob Marshall Country*, *Hiking Colorado's Maroon Bells–Snowmass Wilderness*, *Hiking Glacier and Waterton Lakes National Park*, *Hiking the North Cascades*, *Hiking Olympic National Park*, *Hiking Wyoming's Cloud Peak Wilderness*, and *Wild Wyoming*. He also is the author of *Scenic Driving Alaska and the Yukon* (Globe Pequot Press) and *Alaska on Foot: Wilderness Techniques for the Far North*.

Tamara Martin holds a bachelor of science degree in environmental health from Westchester University in Pennsylvania. After graduation she began her professional career as an environmental consultant in southeast Texas. In pursuit of her dreams, she took a sabbatical to spend a summer hiking in Denali National Park in Alaska. She has also worked as a ranger at Moran State Park in Washington and as a part-time sea-kayaking guide in the San Juan Islands.